INVISIBLE WORLD

INTERIBERICA, S.A. DE EDICIONES

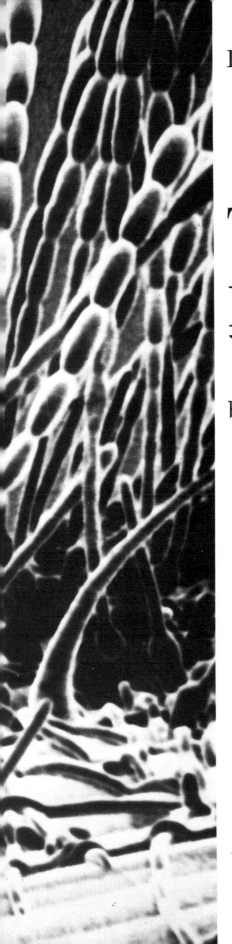

The Living Earth

INVISIBLE WORLD

by Derek Toomer and Alan Cane

ⅅ The Danbury Press

A Division of Grolier Enterprises Inc.

THE DANBURY PRESS
A DIVISION OF GROLIER ENTERPRISES INC.

Publisher: ROBERT B. CLARKE

US ISBN: 0 7172 8104 3
Library of Congress Catalog Card No: 73 9922

© 1975 Interiberica, S.A. - Madrid
© 1975 Aldus Books Limited, London

ISBN: 84-382-0012-5. Dep. Legal: M. 21.865-1975.
Printed and bound in Spain by Novograph
S.A., and Roner S.A., Crta de Irun, Km.12,450,
Madrid–34.

Series Coordinator   Geoffrey Rogers
Art Director   Frank Fry
Design Consultant   Guenther Radtke
Editorial Consultant   Donald Berwick
Series Consultant   Malcolm Ross-Macdonald
Editor   Allyson Rodway
Copy Editors   Maureen Cartwright
Damian Grint
Research   Enid Moore
Peggy Jones
Art Assistants   Vivienne Field
Michael Turner

Contents

Editorial Advisers

DAVID ATTENBOROUGH. Naturalist and Broadcaster.

MICHAEL BOORER, B.SC. Author, Lecturer, and Broadcaster.

MATTHEW BRENNAN, ED.D. Director, Brentree Environmental Center, Professor of Conservation Education, Pennsylvania State University.

PHYLLIS BUSCH, ED.D. Author, Science Teacher, and Consultant in Environmental Education.

MICHAEL HASSELL, B.A., M.A. (OXON), D.PHIL. Lecturer in Ecology, Imperial College, London.

STUART MCNEILL, B.SC., PH.D. Lecturer in Ecology, Imperial College, London.

JAMES OLIVER, PH.D. Director of the New York Aquarium, former Director of the American Museum of Natural History, former Director of the New York Zoological Park, formerly Professor of Zoology, University of Florida.

THE TWENTY VOLUMES IN THE LIVING EARTH SERIES

Introduction

In our urbanized society, many people give hardly a thought to the earth's wildlife or, in fact, to such domesticated organisms as cattle and corn. Our plant and animal foods come prepacked, and we can easily forget the life behind the wrappings. So it is not surprising that we are even less conscious of the existence of a world of living creatures too small to be seen (except perhaps when they erupt as fungus or gather together in vast colonies). If we think of microscopic life forms at all, we tend to characterize them generally as "germs," for among them are some disease-bearing types of bacterium and virus, as well as fungi and algae.

Yet life on this planet would not be possible without the microorganisms. They are essential to the breaking down of dead organic matter so that it can return to the air, sea, and soil; they play a vital role in providing nutrition for plants and in helping herbivorous animals to digest their food; without them we could have neither bread nor cheese; and many of them keep our bodies healthy in strange and wondrous ways even though others do, indeed, cause illness.

From humanity's lofty vantage point, these minute organisms appear to be the lowest forms of life. But we cannot deny that in an evolutionary context they are the most successful of living creatures. They have exploited every possible habitat, including some that would seem highly improbable. Their very simplicity makes them extraordinarily adaptable, able to meet the challenge of changing environments. And so they survive and multiply while more sophisticated life forms stumble toward extinction. It is probable, in fact, that the despised microbes will inherit the earth when all the rest of us have gone. Their invisible world, then, is worth close study, and this volume may well induce some readers to delve more deeply into it.

The Unseen Universe

Familiar sights of land, sea, and air—trees, seaweed, sunset clouds—belong to the world that we know. Over, under, in, and on them live countless tiny creatures whose importance far surpasses their size. See pages 10–11 for a first glimpse of some of the "invisible" inhabitants of these three scenes.

Over the course of millions of years, the living organisms best adapted to the conditions in which they lived have survived and produced descendants; those less well adapted have perished. This inexorable process of natural selection has given rise to the distinctive shapes, forms, and ways of life of all the living things, plant and animal, that we see around us—and to an entire universe of living creatures that are much too tiny to be seen by our unaided eye. Indeed, until powerful magnifying glasses and microscopes were developed in the 17th century, the existence of these strange microorganisms (or microbes, for short) was unknown, and natural clues to their existence—disease, decay,

and alcoholic fermentation—were attributed to magic or divine intervention.

It is with these remarkable microorganisms that this book deals. Despite their size, they are among the most important and interesting of living creatures, with an influence on the earth and its inhabitants that is far out of proportion to their dimensions. Among them are invisible creatures that have drastically changed the course of human history. For example, the bubonic plague, once known as the Black Death, which eliminated a quarter of the population of Europe during the Middle Ages, is caused by a microorganism, a bacterium that we call *Pasteurella pestis*. Other microbes produce a variety of poisonous substances: tetanus, for example, is caused by a powerful poison produced by a bacterium called *Clostridium tetani,* and another bacterium, *Clostridium botulinum*, causes a terrible kind of food poisoning called botulism, which may result in paralysis and death.

But although these examples suggest that microorganisms are chiefly harmful, this is far from the truth. Most of them are beneficial to other living creatures. There is, for instance, a whole range of microorganisms whose activities replenish and enrich the life environment, and on which all living creatures depend ultimately for their survival.

We shall be looking at a few organisms that

we already know well. Mushrooms and toadstools, for example, are the visible clues to the existence of certain kinds of fungus, the other parts of which are invisible to the naked eye. For the most part, however, our tour through the world of microorganisms will be a new and fascinating experience. That is why the names we must use for identifying and describing them are strange. They cannot have common names like "mouse" or "buttercup," because they can be seen only with the aid of a microscope, and so there has never been any need for describing them in familiar terms—apart, that is, from talking vaguely about "germs." The names that identify them are names that make sense primarily to scientists, because scientists are the people who do see and deal with them.

Scientists of all nations use the same scientific

Fertile land has a vast microbial population; in one ounce of good earth there are millions of amoebas like the one below (left). The ocean's plant life appears to be composed mainly of kelp and other large seaweeds—unless, under a microscope, we view the myriad

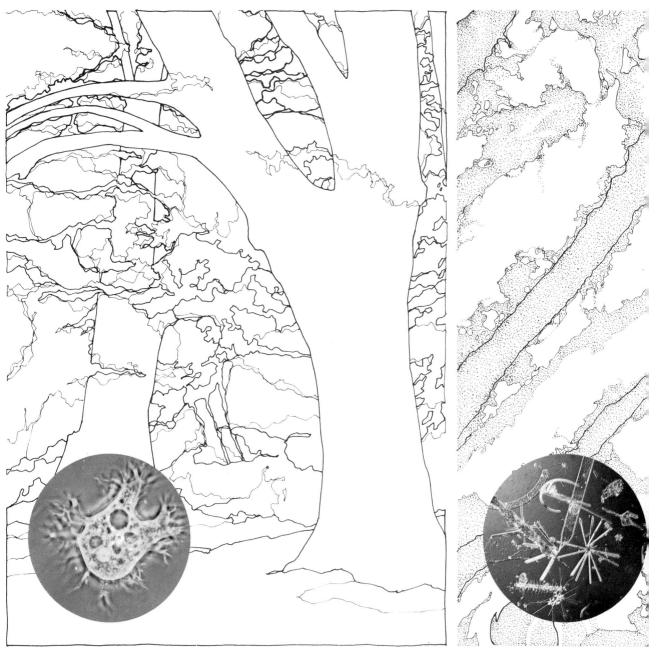

names for all plants and animals. This is for two simple and practical reasons. First, they want to be sure they are talking about the same organisms, and secondly, they choose names that indicate relationships between the many different sorts of creature.

The names of microorganisms are really less intimidating than they look, and it is perfectly possible to appreciate the complexity and excite-

ment of the invisible world without knowing the precise names of all its inhabitants. But it is interesting to know how scientists refer to living organisms—especially because we shall occasionally be using a technical term or two in these pages. Each name consists of two parts. For example, in *Clostridium botulinum,* the food-spoilage organism, *Clostridium* is the generic name: it is used for a number of organisms

algae that make up the phytoplankton (center). Liberated spores of the fungus Puccinia graminis, *seen (right) germinating on a barberry leaf, can be blown hundreds of miles. "Clean" air is often alive with various microorganisms.*

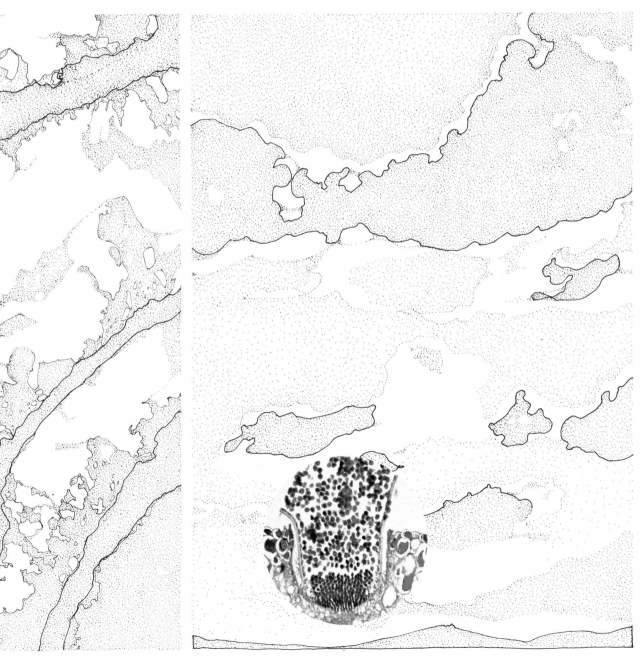

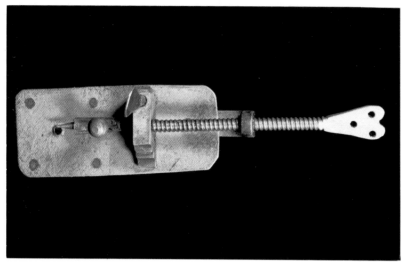

The above ancestor of the electron microscope below has a lens embedded in a metal base; by turning the screw, a viewer could shift an object impaled on its point into viewing position. Primitive? Perhaps. Yet it produced 17th-century drawings such as these at right of two molds, one growing on leather (top), the other on a rose leaf.

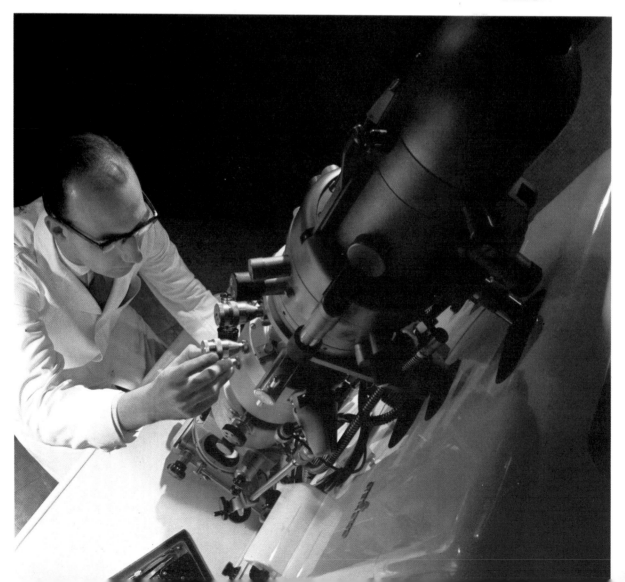

all very much alike but with small distinguishable differences. The generic name is often abbreviated to its capital letter alone. The second name, *botulinum,* refers to a particular kind of *Clostridium* organism. Others are *C. tetani, C. perfringens,* and so on. The same pattern holds for the other creatures of the invisible world (as well as for all visible organisms), with the single exception of the viruses. These—the tiniest and strangest of living things—are often identified simply by code numbers such as PLT22 or T4.

Some scientists believe that microorganisms are the most successful of all living things. It may seem obvious that man, with his ability to find technological answers to most of the problems posed by the climate and geography of the world, is the outstanding success story in the history of this planet. Microorganisms as a group, however, are immensely successful because of their adaptability and variety. The history of antibiotics illustrates how superbly microorganisms adapt in order to overcome adverse changes in their environment. Antibiotics such as penicillin are chemical substances that are extremely effective at killing microorganisms; yet within a few years of the discovery of penicillin and its subsequent widespread use by physicians, there appeared new, penicillin-resistant microbes that caused the same diseases. No matter what antibiotic or combination of antibiotics doctors use, microbes resistant to that antibiotic appear after a time. Even more remarkable is the fact that some microorganisms that acquire resistance to an antibiotic are able to transfer this resistance to other species. That is one reason why the search for new and more effective antibiotics is a chief and extremely important preoccupation of the *pharmaceutical,* or drug-producing, industry.

Man has been able to colonize inhospitable areas of the earth chiefly because of technical and social skill. And like other mammals he can maintain his own body temperature in a wide range of conditions, and the various solutions such as blood, lymph, and so on, that bathe the organs inside his body are kept at just the right consistency. In extreme conditions he constructs defenses to protect himself. Microbes have no sophisticated technical skills, nor can they maintain a constant internal "environment." Yet there is no place on earth that man has colonized where they do not also live. And they inhabit places where neither man nor any other animal or plant could survive.

Because microbes as a whole are so various, they do not form a tight, easily defined group of creatures like, say, the mammals or the fishes, with features in common that distinguish them from other groups. All that the microorganisms have in common is their comparatively simple structure and small size. Whereas higher plants and animals are constructed out of many thousands of cells all working together, a microorganism is only a single cell, or at most a number of single cells joined together in a colony.

The cell is the fundamental unit of which all living organisms are made; and although cells come in many shapes and sizes, every cell is constructed on roughly the same pattern. It is basically a minute blob of jellylike material separated from the outside world by an enveloping membrane, and containing a control center, or *nucleus.* The nucleus not only controls the cell's activities, but also contains the hereditary material that determines what sort of cell it is and what it does.

Many of the cells in higher plants and animals are specialized for particular functions—producing digestive juices, for example, or carrying nerve impulses. Microbes differ in that all their activities are carried out within a single cell or colony of similarly functioning cells. So each microbial cell is, in a sense, equivalent to the entire complicated assemblage of cells that make up the bodies of higher organisms.

In our summary of the invisible world, we shall be looking at five main kinds of microorganism: the protozoans, algae, fungi, bacteria, and viruses. Most members of these groups fit our criteria for inclusion in the invisible world—simplicity of structure and small size—but there are exceptions. We shall not, for example, discuss the larger algae (the seaweeds), fascinating though they are, for they are hardly *micro* organisms; some, indeed, can reach a length of over 100 feet. So we shall concern ourselves only with smaller kinds of algae.

Actually, the word "small" covers a multitude of sizes, for although no microorganism can be seen clearly with the unaided eye, there is a great difference in size between the smallest microorganism and the largest. Because they are all so tiny it is difficult to compare them with anything familiar, and conventional measuring techniques are meaningless. So scientists

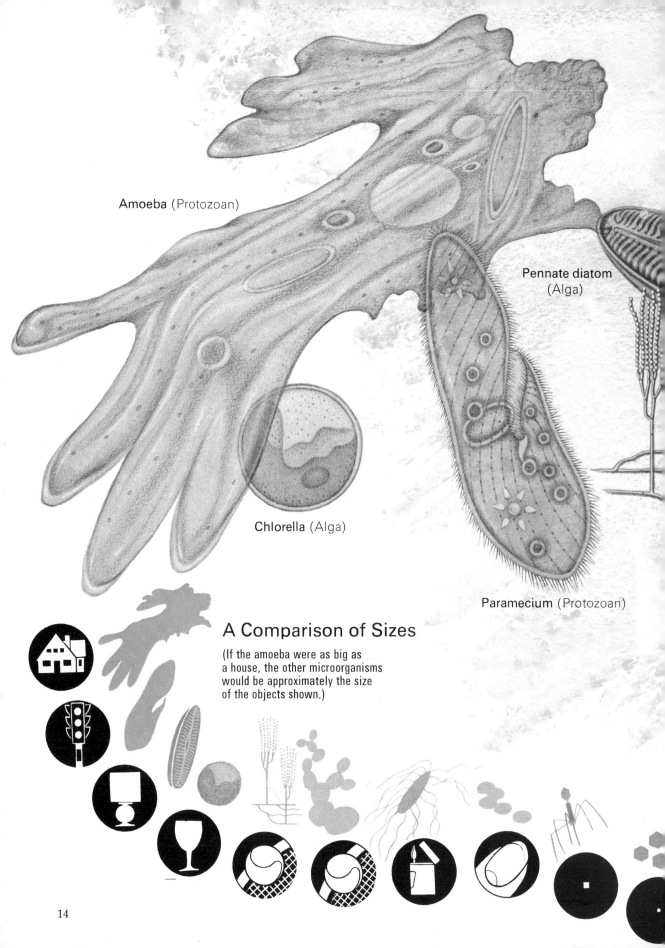

Amoeba (Protozoan)

Pennate diatom
(Alga)

Chlorella (Alga)

Paramecium (Protozoan)

A Comparison of Sizes

(If the amoeba were as big as
a house, the other microorganisms
would be approximately the size
of the objects shown.)

Life-Forms of the Invisible World

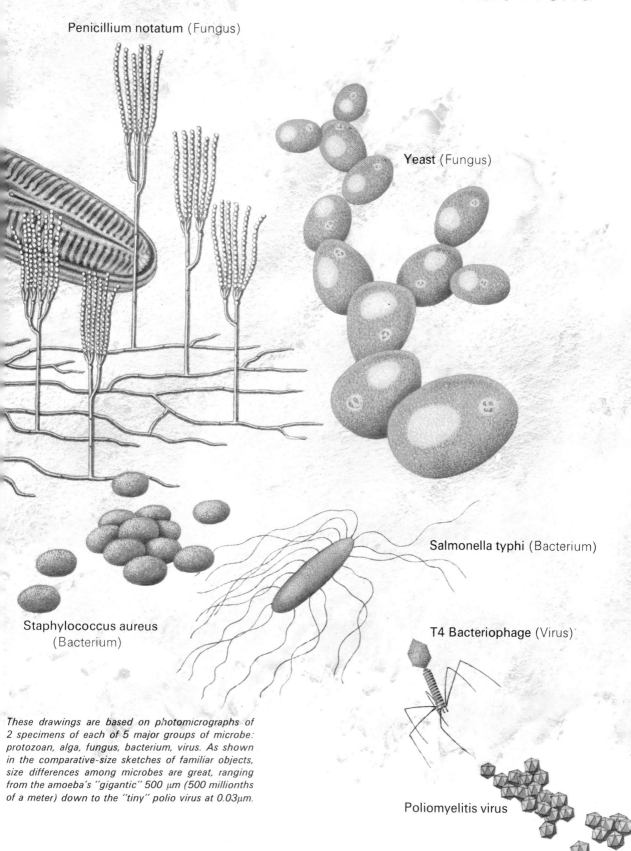

Penicillium notatum (Fungus)

Yeast (Fungus)

Staphylococcus aureus
(Bacterium)

Salmonella typhi (Bacterium)

T4 Bacteriophage (Virus)

These drawings are based on photomicrographs of 2 specimens of each of 5 major groups of microbe: protozoan, alga, fungus, bacterium, virus. As shown in the comparative-size sketches of familiar objects, size differences among microbes are great, ranging from the amoeba's "gigantic" 500 μm (500 millionths of a meter) down to the "tiny" polio virus at 0.03μm.

Poliomyelitis virus

use a special unit for measuring such minute creatures; it is called the micrometer and is written thus: μm. One μm is a millionth part of one meter.

The smallest of all living organisms are the viruses, which may be only 0.03 μm in diameter. Other microorganisms are much larger. Bacteria are usually about one μm in diameter, and the fine threads of fungi may measure as much as five μm across. The giants of the microbial world are the protozoans, some of which, at 500 μm, are just visible as fine specks to the naked eye. Algae come in many different sizes, but the single-celled forms such as *Chlorella* are about 10 μm in diameter.

Few of the microorganisms that we shall be meeting in this book can be classed as either plants or animals, but the algae are clearly true plants, whereas the protozoans are for the most part clearly animals. Plant cells differ from animal cells in that plant cells are surrounded by a rigid wall made of a chemical called *cellulose*. The chief distinction, however, between plants and animals is the fact that green plants make their own food, using the energy of the sun to convert water and carbon dioxide gas into sugar. This process, called *photosynthesis,* is brought about by the pigment chlorophyll, which is found in all green plants. Algae make their food in this way. Protozoans are animal-like in that they must hunt for food. A watery environment is essential to the survival of both.

Protozoans are a very diverse group of organisms. They may live in or on other living creatures, or they may be free-living—that is, they may fend for themselves in nature. There are more than 30,000 known species of these single-celled creatures, most of which have some form of locomotion to help them find food. The different ways in which they move through water serve to distinguish different kinds of protozoan. One group, for example, which

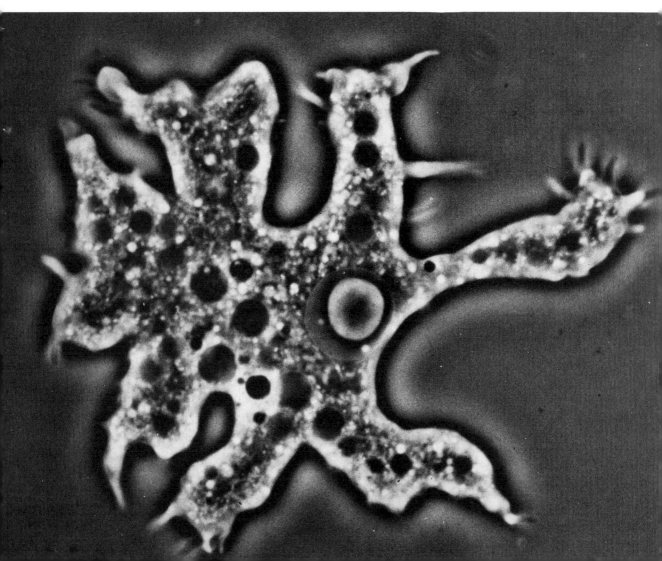

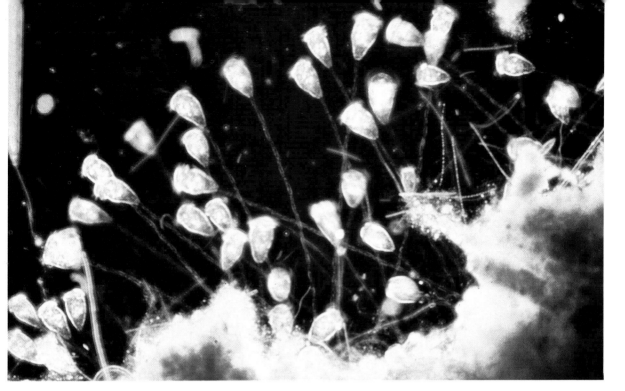

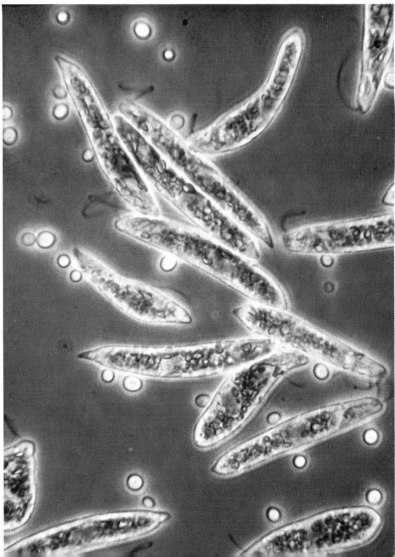

Three of the innumerable varieties of water-dwelling protozoan, which are animal-like in that they move about and hunt for food. An amoeba (left) sends out projections—pseudopodia—that change its shape and keep it flowing along. Vorticellas (above), with their bell-shaped bodies on stems, may resemble plants, but the head can leave its stalk and swim freely, assisted by vibrating cilia. And the long whiplike flagellum protruding from the body of each Euglena (right) helps to propel the organism through the water.

includes the protozoan that causes the disease amoebic dysentery, moves in a manner known as amoeboid movement. The best-known member of this group, *Amoeba proteus,* looks like an irregularly shaped mass of jelly, and moves by sending out flowing projections called *pseudopodia* that change the shape and position of the cell. If the pseudopodia form mainly in one direction the whole amoeba flows that way.

Other protozoans have more sophisticated ways of moving around. For instance, there is a whole group that use long whiplike beaters, known as *flagella,* to propel themselves through the water. Some members of this group—such as the protozoan that causes sleeping sickness in man—have a flagellum that runs the length of their elongated bodies and is attached to an undulating membrane that assists movement. Tiny beaters called *cilia* assist the movement of some protozoans. The cell surface of the slipper-shaped *Paramecium* is covered with cilia, which are much shorter than flagella. Paramecia are unusual in that they have a definite "mouth" region at one side of the cell, and the cilia around the mouth are especially modified to create a vortex in the water to pull food particles into the mouth as the paramecium cell moves along.

But not all protozoans have a means of propulsion. For example, for the major part of its life cycle the protozoan that causes malaria merely floats in the bloodstream, absorbing food through its cell wall. Some protozoans even build houses around their naked cells. The amoebalike creatures called *foraminiferans* secrete shells of chalk or silica, often of great beauty, around themselves. *Foraminifera* means "holebearers,' a name that refers to the numerous holes in their shells through which they send out long jellylike strands of protoplasm to capture food particles from around them.

Like the protozoans, algae need a watery habitat. They differ in that they are green plants and can create their food photosynthetically. The simplest of the many kinds of algae are free-living, single-celled organisms that move by thrashing two whiplike flagella. In this they resemble the free-living, single-celled protozoans, and, indeed, at this level of simplicity only the presence of chlorophyll serves to separate the plants from the animals. Why should algae have any need of movement, if they do not have to hunt for food? The answer is that they must "hunt" for sunlight.

In more complex algae, many flagella-equipped cells may be associated in a spherical colony. The flagella from *each* cell are directed to the outside of the sphere, and the colony rolls through the water as a result of their coordinated beating. Each cell in such a colony is, of course, microscopic in size; the colony itself is only the size of a pinhead. Many algae have no means of movement, especially those that consist of long filaments of cells joined end to end. *Spirogyra*—a colony of algae readily recognized because the chlorophyll is contained in a distinctive spiral-shaped structure inside each cell, like a green spring—is of this kind. One end of its filament is generally tethered to a rock or to another plant in quiet fresh water, and the rest of it floats.

The mainly free-floating algae known as *diatoms* are found worldwide—in seas, in fresh water, and in moist soil. The characteristic feature of a diatom is its hard siliceous cell wall, which surrounds the alga like a box. These hard walls are finely sculptured into remarkably beautiful patterns, but they are so small that it takes a microscope to reveal their full splendor.

Often considered with the algae, but not strictly related to them, are the blue-green algae. (The name comes from the combination of blue and green pigments in their cells.) These microorganisms, which include single-celled and filamentous forms, occur in a wide range of habitats, including extreme environmental situations such as saline lakes and desert soils. They are not classified with true algae because their cells are relatively simple in structure; they lack distinct nuclei, for example. They therefore form a separate group whose exact position in the evolutionary development of other microorganisms is still being investigated by microbiologists.

So far we have taken a preliminary look at organisms—the algae and the protozoans—that are at least recognizably akin to familiar plants and animals. Now let us meet some groups of microbes that are quite unlike anything we know in the visible world. The first such group comprises the invisible parts of the fungi. Fungi are rather like green plants in that their cells are

Though single-celled, the slipper-shaped Paramecium *has a very complex structure, the outer surface of which is covered with tiny beaters called cilia. These paramecia have been highly stained to show the nucleus (blue) and numerous cavities, or* vacuoles, *in which food particles (red) are enclosed for digestion.*

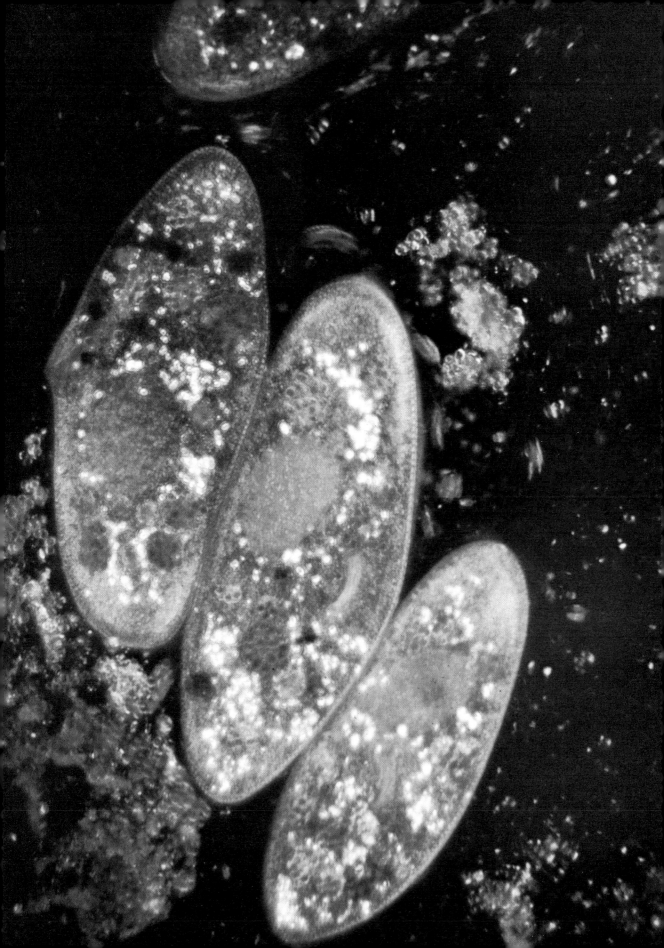

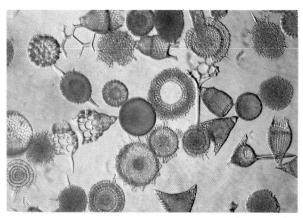

surrounded by a rigid cell wall; but whereas plant cell walls are stiffened with cellulose, fungal cell walls are stiffened with another chemical, chitin, which is similar to the hard substance that covers and protects the bodies of insects. The fungi are unlike familiar plants in that they have no chlorophyll and are thus unable to build up their own food substances from simple chemicals. Like animals, they must depend on ready-made food, whether dead or alive.

Thus the fungi are either *parasites* (that is, living in or on other living organisms) or *saprophytes* (living on dead or decaying organic

Right: the White Cliffs of Dover in England are composed of masses upon masses of microscopic shells—the incredibly varied and often lovely "houses" that the foraminiferan protozoans build around themselves. These shells sank to the bottom of the sea when the foraminifers died, and formed a thick layer; later changes in sea level exposed this to the air. As seen in these specimens (pink-stained in the top photograph, green-stained in the bottom one), the shells of the foraminifers, which are mostly marine creatures, are perforated with minute holes, through which protrude strands of protoplasm for capturing food.

matter). Many of the saprophytes, and some parasites, produce mushrooms and toadstools—the fruiting bodies that the fungus sends up above the ground to disperse its *spores* (reproductive cells that will give rise to new individuals). The main body of the fungus consists of a fine network of branching colorless threads, or *hyphae,* that form a system called the *mycelium.* The mycelium, which grows on the substance from which the fungus draws its nourishment, is often invisible to the naked eye.

Parasitic fungi also produce mycelia, and these can eventually kill the host. One fungal parasite, for example, lives on the common housefly; its spores adhere to the insect's body, and on germination they sprout fine tubes that pierce the skin and bud off roundish cells inside its body, each of which develops into a mycelium. In time the fly dies, choked with fungal threads.

The housefly parasite belongs to the smallest and most primitive class of fungi. Among the 1000 or so species in this class are the water molds, which cause the fringes of colorless, threadlike hyphae seen on dead fish or other once-living material floating in lakes and canals. Also in the group are the parasitic fungi that are

responsible for the disease of downy mildew in many plants and the saprophytic fungi that make damp bread or fruit moldy.

The largest class of fungi, with almost 30,000 species, is distinguished by a special kind of spore-producing unit, the *ascus,* in which the spores develop in a long file before being liberated into the air. This group includes the fungi that produce the brilliant orange structures found on rotting wood or on the forest floor. It also includes the below-ground species *Tuber,* which produce the edible truffles highly prized by gourmets. And another member of the group, of immense importance to nearly everyone in the world, is yeast—or, rather, the various yeasts that are essential for brewing and baking.

The second largest fungal category includes about 13,000 species, among them all those saprophytes that send up fruiting bodies: the toadstools, bracket fungi, puffballs, and stinkhorns. Also in this class are many tiny fungi, including the dreaded food-crop parasites the rusts and smuts. All these fungi are identified collectively by the production of a characteristically shaped spore-producing structure, called the *basidium.*

The last group of fungi is actually composed of several kinds, which, because they seem to belong to no precise category, are lumped together under the catchall name of Fungi Imperfecti. Among these "imperfect" microorganisms are the fungi that cause such skin diseases in man as ringworm and athlete's foot. And there are also some microorganisms that, although not true fungi, are frequently included in the group: the slime molds. At certain stages a slime mold resembles nothing so much as a smear of white or colored jelly. Often to be found on fallen tree trunks and branches, slime molds feed on decaying plant matter such as rotting wood, leaf litter, and even old bracket fungi. It is rather like a mass of amoeboid creatures combined into one slimy sheet of jelly without any barrier membranes between the individual cells. The characteristic that slime molds have in common with the fungi is that they are able to produce complex and often colorful fruiting bodies to disperse spores.

We now turn to what is probably the most significant group of microorganisms: the bacteria. These are extremely simple, single-celled organisms, which may be spherical or oval, rod-shaped, filamentous (threadlike), spiral, or vibrioid (shaped like a comma). They may be found in chains, clusters, or pairs of cells.

The structure of the bacteria is simpler than that of any other group of organisms except the viruses, which are not even true cells. A bacterial cell, although it *is* a cell, is unlike, say, a protozoan or an alga in that it does not have a true nucleus. Each cell is surrounded by a relatively thick and rigid cell wall, which may have a coating of gelatinous material, the capsule, with a probably protective function. Many species have one or more flagella by which they move, and these may be concentrated at one end of the cell or arranged in a variety of ways.

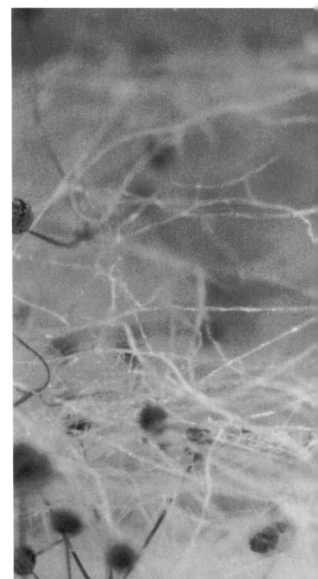

Flourishing on moldy bread is the cobwebby mycelium of the fungus Rhizopus *(common bread mold), with its spherical spore sacs rising into the air. Released spores of this fungus are everywhere, ready to germinate on damp organic material.*

Their structure is a poor aid to classification, and so to naming, although oval-shaped bacteria are appropriately called *cocci,* from the Greek word for "seeds," and rod-shaped bacteria are also appropriately termed *bacilli,* from the Latin for "little staffs." For the most part, however, characteristics other than shape and structure are used as guides to describing and naming the various species. Thus there are lactic-acid bacteria, which can ferment milk-sugar, and iron bacteria, which derive their energy by a chemical reaction involving iron; there are enteric bacteria, which live in the intestines of man and other animals; there are also gliding bacteria, photosynthetic bacteria, and so on. They can also be divided into two groups, Gram-negative and Gram-positive, depending on whether they can be stained with a dye developed by the Danish bacteriologist Christian Gram.

This rather condensed recital of the physical characteristics of bacteria gives no hint of the diverse nature of their activities or of their importance. The most fundamental and far-reaching characteristic of bacteria is their ability to survive and multiply.

No other microorganisms are as prolific as the bacteria, which multiply extremely rapidly by dividing. Some species reproduce themselves so quickly that a single bacterium can give rise to over a million offspring in a few hours. There is also a process of sexual reproduction; the "male" and "female" bacteria come together (the sexes are physically identical, but they play different roles in mating), and part of the hereditary material of the male passes to the female through a bridge of living material that develops between them. The two partners then separate, and both begin to divide. But only the cells derived from

the "female" bacterium show combinations of the characteristics inherited from both parents.

Bacteria do not produce spores for reproduction. But they sometimes produce endospores, which are spherical or oval structures inside the bacterial cell. Brought forth only in unfavorable conditions, these are the most resistant living things known. They can survive drying out, disinfectants, and extremely high temperatures.

It is appropriate here to look at the variety of reproduction methods in the other groups of microorganisms. With the exception of the viruses, all of them follow much the same pattern as the bacteria: they multiply by division.

Although many protozoans simply divide, there is a primitive kind of sexual reproduction in most species, which transfers hereditary material from one protozoan to another. In *Paramecium*,

for example, there are two nuclei, one large, one small, to each cell. The larger nucleus, whose job is chiefly to control the coordination of the free-living cell, disintegrates when one paramecium cell comes into close contact with another. The remaining nucleus in each of the paramecia divides into four, three of which degenerate, leaving only one. This divides into two, and one of these is exchanged between the partners. The two pieces of nucleus in each

Because they lack a supply of chlorophyll, fungi cannot manufacture their own food, but are forced to depend on external substances, whether dead or alive. Some, such as those below, are saprophytes: that is, they eat decaying plant or animal matter—for example, the bark of a dead tree (left) or sheep's dung (right). Other fungi are parasitic; as their fungal threads branch out, they progressively infect the host, as in mildewed fruit (right), and perhaps even eventually kill it, as in the mycelium-choked housefly (far right).

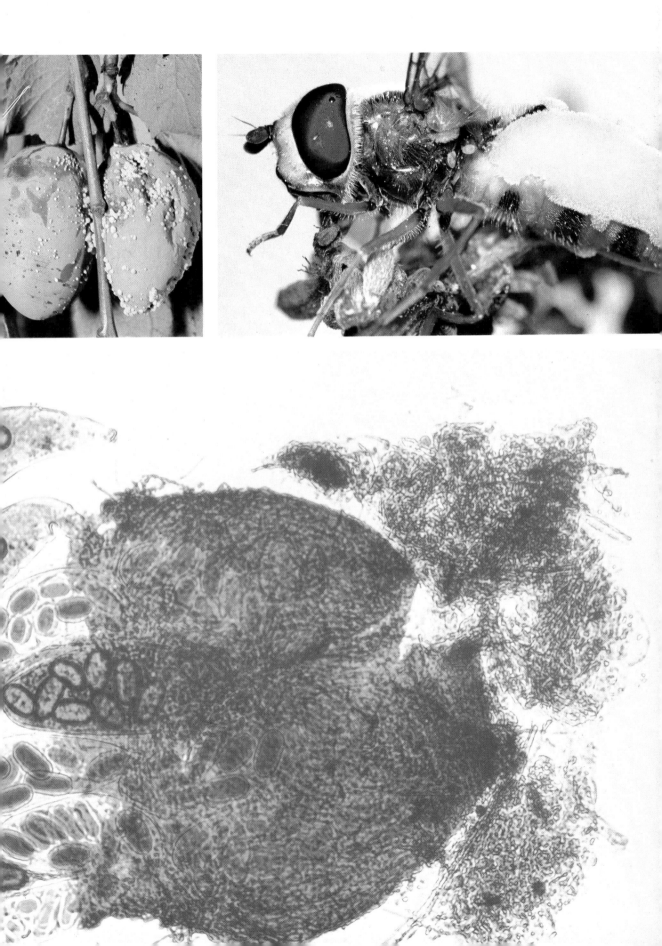

partner now fuse, and the paramecia separate. The new composite nucleus in each of them divides into four, and the paramecium itself divides in half, with two nuclei to each new cell. Thus four paramecia have been formed from the original two, with a mutual exchange of hereditary material. Some protozoans also form spores—roughly spherical structures with hard, resistant walls—which can remain alive during bad conditions and give rise to new protozoans when conditions improve.

In the algae and fungi, multiplication by division of a single cell is only one of a number of ways of reproduction. Division can also occur through the cutting off of a new part of the filament in a filamentous alga or fungus. In most of these microorganisms, though, some kind of sexual reproduction takes place. The spores produced in the asci and basidia of the fungi that possess such structures are the result of sexual reproduction.

With the viruses, we come to the smallest and some of the simplest of all living things, and also to the strangest type of microbial reproduction. Carl Linnaeus, the 18th-century Swedish biologist who devised the system of scientific names that we now use to classify living things, described three natural kingdoms, animal, plant, and mineral. If he had known about viruses, he would have been hard-pressed to decide which of his three kingdoms they should be assigned to. They live only in other living organisms—in plants and animals, and some, the so-called *bacteriophages,* in bacteria. "Live" is perhaps a rather questionable word, because they exhibit none of the usual properties that we think of as denoting life.

The whole existence of the viruses is devoted to the production of more viruses. To do this, they invade living cells and ultimately destroy them. Once inside a cell, they take control of its nucleus and divert it from its normal function to the task of manufacturing and assembling new viruses. They cause a range of diseases of varying degrees of severity; in human beings, for instance, viral infection brings on such complaints as the common cold and smallpox.

Viruses have been described as "living chemicals," and they are often, in fact, barely distinguishable from mere chemicals. Some of the smaller ones—for example, the one that causes mosaic disease of the leaf in tobacco plants—can be crystallized from solution in the same

way as common salt crystals. But the virus loses little of its potency through such drastic treatment. If dissolved again and injected into a healthy tobacco plant, it will again cause the same mosaic disease.

Despite their extreme simplicity, these mysterious organisms have a distinct structure, which the superior power of the electron microscope reveals. Some, for example, are geometrical structures called *icosahedrons*—that is, they have 20 triangular faces and 12 corners. Bacteriophages, the viruses that live on bacteria,

The slime molds, though not actually fungi, resemble the fungi in their ability to produce fruiting bodies for the dispersal of their spores. To the naked eye, the masses of single-celled creatures that combine into visible slime molds look like smears of white or colored jelly as they flow along decaying plant matter such as damp logs or leaf litter. Under the microscope, however, we get a clear view of their spore cases (technically called sporangia*), as in these colorful photographs of green, yellow, and brown varieties of slime mold.*

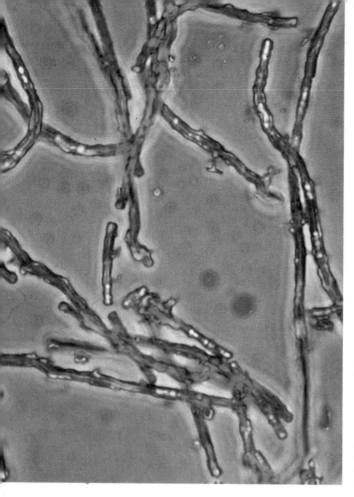

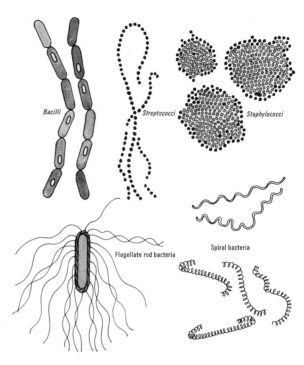

Above: five of the many types of bacterium, which are often named according to their shapes: the bacilli, for example, are rod-shaped (Latin bacillum means "little staff"), and the cocci are spherical (from the Greek for "seed"). Left: when these anthrax bacilli attack cattle or sheep, the infection is usually fatal, and it can even be transmitted to man.

have a head, a tail, and an irregular array of tail fibers. Some viruses, such as the tobacco mosaic virus, appear as long rods with a coiled spring-like center. Whatever their shape, however, all of them are little more than bundles of hereditary material surrounded by a coat of protein.

Now that we have seen something of the kinds of creatures that inhabit the invisible world, we shall now discover something of their activities. Only in comparatively recent times have microscopes been powerful enough to show us these tiny creatures in action; but some of the shrewder early biologists suspected that something more than supernatural powers was involved in phenomena such as the souring of milk and the onset of disease. In the 1600s, lens-making techniques were sufficiently advanced to allow Anton van Leeuwenhoek, a Dutchman, to make the first investigation of microbial life. It was a profound experience for him. "What if one should tell people in future that there are more animals living in the scum of the teeth in a man's mouth than there are men

in a whole kingdom!" he wrote musingly. And now microorganisms have been found not only on men's teeth but in every conceivable environmental niche—and also in quite a number that are hardly conceivable at all.

Most living creatures cannot survive extremes of heat or cold. At very high temperatures, the complicated chemicals that are essential for life are destroyed, and at low temperatures the chemical reactions required to provide energy for growth take place too slowly to support life. Nevertheless, some microorganisms are able to live and grow at the freezing point of water (32°F). Particularly spectacular examples are the algae that grow on the surface of Arctic snowfields in such profusion that they color the snow red or green. Furthermore, freezing does not necessarily kill bacteria. Proof of this is shown by the fact that when samples of frozen human waste taken recently from huts used in 1913 by the British Antarctic explorer Sir Ernest Shackleton were thawed, they yielded living intestinal-bacterial cells.

Some bacteria, too, can tolerate extreme

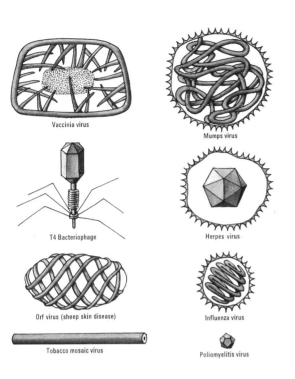

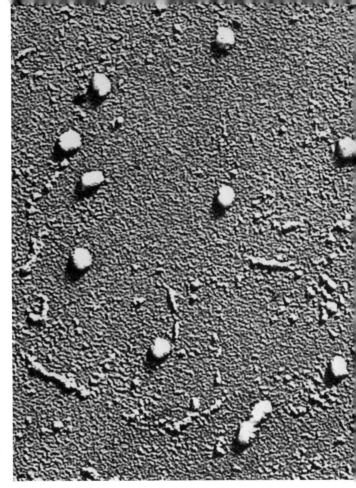

Above: although the viruses are the smallest of all the microbes, these "living chemicals" have distinct, and often remarkably complex, structures. This is what a few of them look like when examined through an electron microscope. Right: an actual photomicrograph of particles of the spherical virus that causes influenza, a common ailment of man.

Labels in illustration:
Vaccinia virus
Mumps virus
T4 Bacteriophage
Herpes virus
Orf virus (sheep skin disease)
Influenza virus
Tobacco mosaic virus
Poliomyelitis virus

heat. The best-known examples live around the boiling springs that can be found in several parts of the world. There are over 10,000 such springs in Yellowstone National Park, Wyoming, where the temperature of the issuing water is nearly 200°F. Yet rod-shaped bacteria are to be found growing and multiplying on the rocks washed by the steamy waters. And the endospores of some species of bacteria can withstand continuous boiling for several minutes, a treatment that would destroy most other forms of life.

In the absence of water, however, even the hardiest microorganism cannot grow and multiply. But many can withstand extreme desiccation. For instance, living bacteria have been grown from spores preserved in dried 17th-century plant specimens. Microorganisms have also been found at extreme depths and heights. Some have been detected flourishing in the sediment at the bottom of the seven-mile-deep Pacific trench, and at the other end of the scale, American spacemen have found fungal spores several miles up in the stratosphere. There are also bacteria that can resist attack by what are to us poisons and dangerous chemicals. Some species actually produce sulfuric acid from sulfur compounds, and others have been found growing in conditions of extreme alkalinity.

All of this indicates the measure of the extraordinary success of microorganisms as living creatures. They can thrive in some of the unfriendliest environments on earth. Many microorganisms are entirely dependent for their survival on the creatures they live with or in, and they have to be adapted to life in their willing or unwilling hosts in much the same way that bacteria around natural hot springs must be modified to withstand the continual dousing with boiling water.

For some microorganisms, the relationship with the host is wholly destructive. The parasitic bacteriophages, for example, use their bacterial hosts merely as a factory for reproducing themselves; once finished, they leave the gutted hulk in search of new cells to capture. But there are many, many ways in which organisms can live in association with one another, and most of these are beneficial to one or both

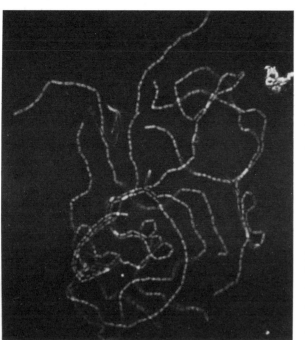

of the partners. We have already mentioned parasitism and saprophytism in relation to fungi, but there is also *symbiosis*: the prolonged, close, and often profitable association of different species. An example is that of the green algae that live within protozoans: the algae gain mobility and shelter, while the protozoans gain whatever excess food the algae manufacture. Another very common form of association is *commensalism*, where, although all the benefits go to one of the partners, the other is not harmed in any way by the relationship.

In the pages that follow we shall see how the five types of microorganism live, and find their nourishment, and we shall try to understand the part they play in ensuring that the elements vital to life on earth are kept continually in circulation. We shall see also how the various kinds of invisible beings have become adapted to living in association, both loose and intimate, with other living creatures.

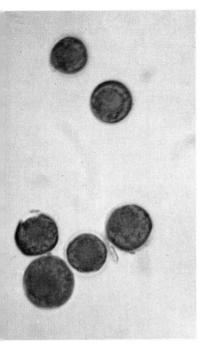

No other living creatures can compete with the microorganisms in their ability to survive in the most inhospitable of environments. They thrive not only in every likely place but also in places where almost no other life could exist. Rocks around Minerva Spring in Yellowstone National Park (left) are continuously washed by steaming water at nearly 200°F; yet rod-shaped bacteria like those at the top of the opposite page grow and multiply there. At the other end of the thermometer, in the freezing heights of the Cascade Range of Oregon, there are so many red-pigmented alga spores (similar to those isolated above in a highly magnified picture) that the snow itself looks red. The red snow shown at right is the result of a profusion of resting spores. The snow turns green when many alga cells are in the growth rather than the resting stage.

Free-Living Microbes

Without the unique abilities and activities of microorganisms, life on earth would soon grind to a halt, for microbes supply vitally needed building materials to living organisms. We live in a world where the essential materials of life are in limited supply; if the materials that provide growth and energy for one generation were to remain imprisoned in their bodies after death, there would be a severe shortage of resources for succeeding generations. Life continues to exist because these materials are recycled. When a plant or animal dies, its remains are pillaged for food by bacteria and other microorganisms, which break down the dead tissue, reduce the materials from which it is constructed to simpler forms, and eventually return them to the environment for further use.

It is chiefly the free-living microorganisms that maintain these natural cycles of growth and decay. Free-living microorganisms are those whose evolutionary path has led them into a life style in which they must find their food in open competition with other forms of life. They do this efficiently because of their versatility and their ability to colonize new environments and to use all sorts of chemicals as food. So now let us consider a few examples of these invisible creatures in search of food.

Protozoans must hunt and catch their food. Thus they need some way to move about; and, as we saw in Chapter 1, they are equipped with a variety of means of movement. Some protozoans—the amoebalike species—both feed and move by means of the same mechanism. They engulf their food as they flow along, surrounding it with protoplasm and incorporating it into the cell. The food may well be a bacterium, which becomes enclosed inside the protozoan together with a small drop of the water in which it has been swimming. Digestive juices are then secreted into this vacuole to break down the food into simpler substances.

The only visible life on this rotting carcass of a horse is a butterfly, which has alighted there for a brilliant moment. But the very word "rotting" implies another kind of life; dead flesh rots because it is alive with microorganisms that break down the tissue and recycle it into the environment.

Protozoans attack and devour other protozoans as well as bacteria. One, *Didinium,* is a voracious and resourceful killer of the protozoan *Paramecium,* and biologists have made a detailed study of the way it hunts, captures, and kills its quarry. A hungry *Didinium* swims through the water with the aid of its fringelike cilia in a more or less straight line until it collides—by chance, it seems—with a *paramecium.* The prey is at least as large as the hunter, but on collision the *Didinium* "harpoons" its victim by firing "spears" into it. Some are fired with such force that they are torn away from the *Didinium;* others remain attached. The "spears" apparently contain a poison that first paralyzes and then kills the *paramecium.* The *Didinium* hauls back its harpoons, dragging the victim along with them, and so into its mouth. Once the prey is engulfed, the much-distended *Didinium* swims off to digest its meal. All this complicated weaponry and mechanism, remember, exists in an organism whose body is *only a single cell.*

As we saw in the last chapter, the fungi cannot manufacture their own food. Many live, therefore, as parasites in or on living creatures and we shall come to those in later chapters. The free-living members of the fungi, however, feed on dead organic matter. For instance, the common green mold *Penicillium* and the common black mold *Aspergillus* will grow happily on anything from strawberry jam to shoe leather. All they need in addition is a little moisture. Fungi are particularly adept at using dead wood as a source of nourishment. The network of fine threads can make its way inside a decaying tree trunk or a fallen branch in a manner that is quite impossible for the smaller, less complicated bacteria. The threads make their way through the woody tissue of the dead tree, passing from cell to cell and digesting the substance of the cell walls. When a forest tree is felled, fungi start to colonize the cut surface of the stump immediately, and particular kinds of tree are colonized by specific fungi. A beech stump, for instance, will soon bear examples of several different species— some purple, some orange, some black and tarlike—whereas oak wood is attacked by comparatively few, perhaps because of its high tannin content. Coniferous wood also has a distinctive flora, including the orange gelatinous fungus *Calocera viscosa.*

Sometimes fungi that can live on either dead or living wood use a dead tree stump as a base from which to send out "creepers" to infect the roots of nearby living trees. The results can be so devastating that woodsmen occasionally encourage harmless fungi to colonize cut stumps to keep out the dangerous species.

Microorganisms help to return vital building materials to the living world not only by decomposing dead tissue but also by breaking down animal wastes. Freshly deposited dung is quickly colonized by a succession of bacteria and fungi. Certain fungi also feed on the eelworms that flourish in old dung or in rotten wood, and they have ingenious methods of trapping their prey. One type of fungus creates three-dimensional labyrinths—networks of fine fungal threads coated with a strongly adhesive substance; the eelworm enters the maze, becomes irretrievably stuck, and soon dies of exhaustion and hunger. Another type sets a trap rather like a noose-snare; when an eelworm enters the trap, the cells that make up the noose inflate suddenly, holding the worm in a viselike grip.

Now that we have seen something of the feeding habits of individual decomposers (as microbes that help in the breakdown of living or once-living tissue are called) let us take a specific example of how they work together to return vital nutrients to the soil.

A leaf falls from a tree at the end of summer. Swiftly it is invaded by the growing threads of various microscopic fungi, which may have been growing in the soil already or may germinate from spores lying dormant there. As the fungi begin to digest away the substance of the leaf, bacteria arrive for their share of the spoils; they feed not only on the matter of the leaf itself, but also on the waste products left by the fungi as they wind their way through the leaf. All this uninhibited feasting requires energy, however, and the fungi and bacteria that initiated the process of decomposition need oxygen as well as food for the production of energy. Oxygen may become scarce within the tissues of the leaf, as it is used up by the initial invaders, the fungi and bacteria, and so other kinds of microorganisms that do not need oxygen can take over. These produce acidic substances as they feed on the

By decomposing dead tissues, the microorganisms help to return vital building materials to the living world. In this linear representation of the photograph on page 33, the circular inset shows in magnified form what the naked eye cannot see: vast numbers of bacteria feeding on decaying flesh.

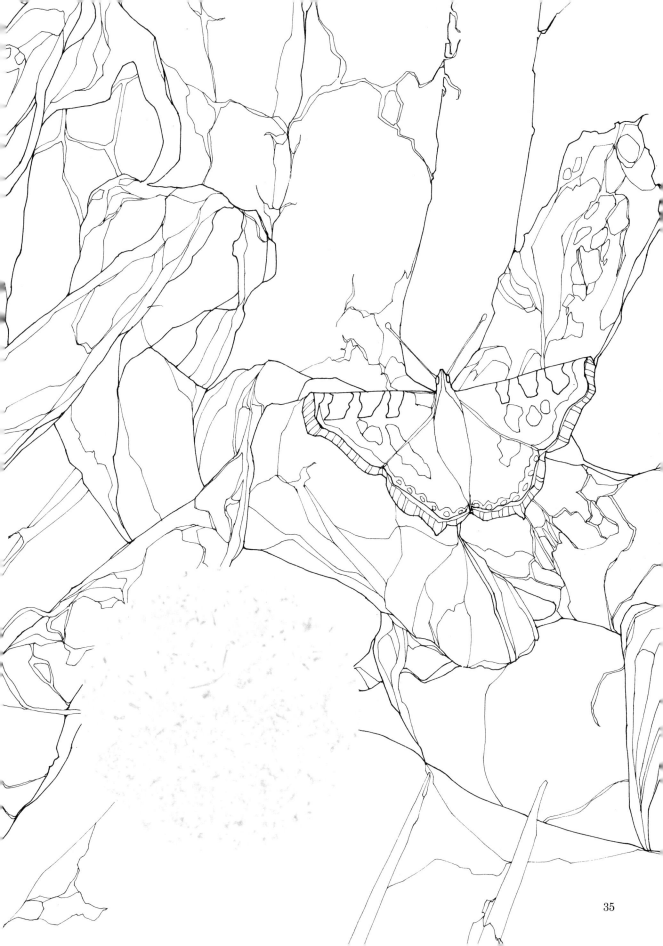

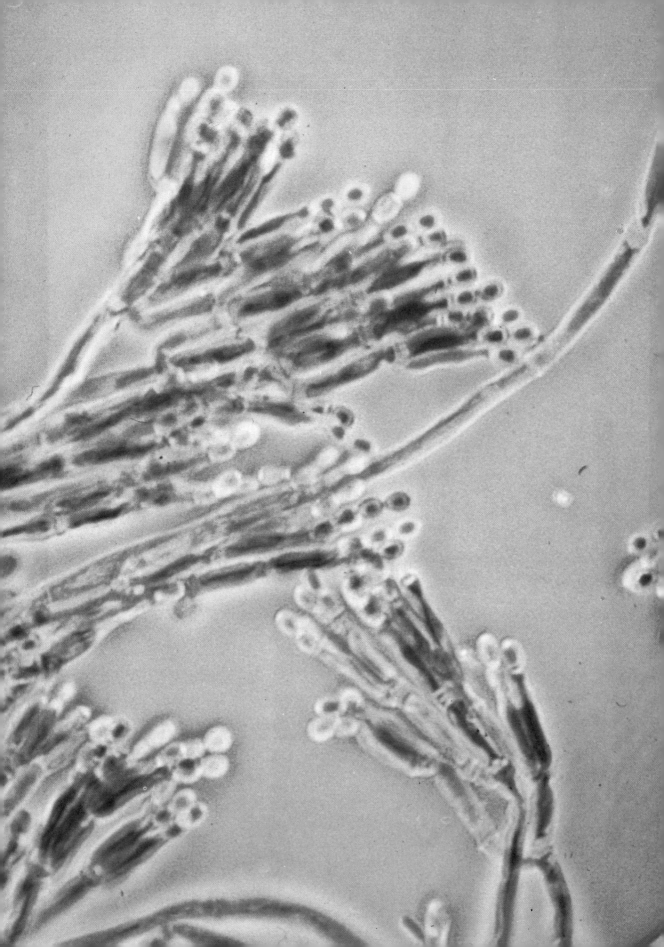

leaf tissues. So yet another group of microbes, which can use these particular acids as food, can now join in the banquet.

While the bacteria have been feeding, protozoans grazing in the film of water on the leaf surface have been consuming the bacteria. Larger soil animals such as earthworms, woodlice, earwigs, and termites help to tear the leaf into smaller pieces, many of which become incorporated in the top layers of the soil. Eventually, all the leaf is decomposed and its substance carried into the topsoil or bound into the bodies of microorganisms, which die in their turn and are decomposed in the soil or eaten by other creatures. And so the life-making substances once locked into the leaf are redistributed. There is a very old saying that "corruption is the mother of vegetation"—proving that long before they discovered the presence of microorganisms, farmers recognized that what makes the difference between fertility and infertility is the soil's capacity to release the vital nutrients from dead remains.

One of the most important differences, in fact, between a fertile soil and a mere accumulation of rock particles is the presence in the soil of a thriving microbial population. A fertile soil is either well supplied from the beginning with nutrients in a form that green plants can use, or rich in microorganisms able to unlock the vital nutrients from dead organic remains. Man, of course, makes use of the decomposing abilities of microorganisms in preparing compost—rotted-down heaps of animal and vegetable remains are added to the soil to improve its fertility.

Soil bacteria live chiefly on the surface of the particles that make up the soil, and they adhere tightly to these surfaces. They are present in

Mold, like that on the quince below, is formed by the air spores of free-living saprophytic fungi. One such species, Penicillium *(left), produces penicillin, whose power to kill certain disease-bearing bacteria has proved a boon to medicine.*

very large numbers. Recent measurements suggest that soil from arable land may contain over 100,000 million bacteria in each ounce. Agriculturalists have calculated that if they average this number throughout the top six inches of soil, and if the top six inches weigh about 1000 tons an acre, there may be between 0.6 and 1.5 tons of living bacteria in every acre of good earth. Moreover, representatives of all the other types of microorganism also live in the soil. Some indication of the vast numbers of these simple forms of life is the authoritative calculation that for every 300 million bacteria in good soils there are 3 million fungi and over 60 million other microorganisms, including protozoans and blue-green algae.

One group of soil organisms that we have not yet discussed is the actinomycetes. In some ways these free-living creatures are like bacteria, but in others they resemble the fungi. They form fine, many-branched networks of microscopic threads in the soil, and they produce a substance that scientists term "geosmin," which is responsible for the characteristic musty odor of newly turned earth. A typical example of a soil actinomycete is *Streptomyces*. Perhaps the most striking characteristic of this microbe, and of its near relatives, is the fact that it produces an antibiotic—a substance that kills or prevents the growth of other microorganisms. We shall see in a later chapter how we use this substance, called *streptomycin,* as a weapon against disease.

So far we have seen free-living microorganisms at work chiefly as demolition experts; now let us look at them as creators of the building-bricks of life. Nitrogen, a constituent of protein, is one such building-brick. Although nitrogen is the most abundant gas in the atmosphere, plants and animals cannot incorporate it directly into their protein. Plants can absorb it from the soil only in a watery solution, as a salt of ammonia or as nitrate. Bacteria release ammonia and nitrates into the soil through the decomposition of dead remains, but they also free nitrogen that is imprisoned in plant or animal remains and release it as a gas. Through this process and through *leaching*—whereby rainwater, in draining through the top layers of soil, carries soluble mineral salts down beyond the reach of plant roots—soils are continually being depleted of nitrogen. Soils that support commercial crops also lose nitrogen, of course, because the harvested crop takes a good deal away.

Some nitrogen in the form of nitrates and ammonia is returned to the soil in rainwater—up to five pounds an acre in one year, according to measurements made at Cornell University in New York State. But that is hardly enough to compensate for the amounts lost in other ways. What does make up for the loss is the activities of soil microorganisms that convert gaseous nitrogen into soluble nitrogen-containing substances that can be absorbed by plant roots and turned into protein. Because green plants are the primary producers of food for the majority of living creatures, the importance of such microorganisms cannot be overestimated.

The most important way in which this conversion occurs is through bacteria that live in special parts of the root—the root nodules—of leguminous plants such as peas and beans. But this is in a special kind of association that we shall be discussing in Chapter 3. There are free-living organisms, however, that do fix atmospheric nitrogen. The list of such organisms includes some bacteria and a few yeasts, but the most important contribution to the overall exchange of nitrogen between the living and nonliving worlds results from the activities of certain species of blue-green algae.

In tropical climates, blue-green algae may fix as much as 70 pounds of nitrogen a year for every acre. They abound in the waters of the paddy fields of Southeast Asia, and that fact is of considerable significance to rice growers. In temperate climates, colonies of blue-green algae are found in shallow marine bays where the water is warm, in freshwater lakes where nutrients are freely available, and in the soil. Dark, nearly black patches on the damp surface of the soil in gardens and in flowerpots in greenhouses are almost certain to be the variety of blue-green alga called *Nostoc*.

Because they contain chlorophyll, blue-green algae can manufacture their own food. With this self-sufficiency and with their remarkable resistance to bad conditions, they are often the first form of life to colonize a new habitat. For example, they appeared on the rocks and volcanic ash of the Indonesian island of Krakatoa within three years of the devastating volcanic eruption of 1883, which blew off the entire top of the island and destroyed all its visible life. More recently, between 1963 and 1967, when further violence within the earth's crust threw up the island of Surtsey off the south coast of Iceland, the

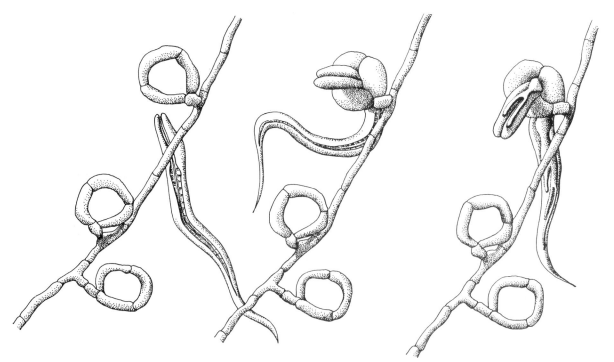

How one type of soil-dwelling fungus snares living prey: the mold forms a sticky network of loops, into which an unwary eelworm blunders; the trap is sprung as the loop's three cells expand and hold the worm in a firm grip; after hours of struggle, the victim dies and is digested by branching filaments of its captor.

barren surface of the new land became the home of blue-green algae within a year.

Nitrogen fixation is by far the most important process through which microorganisms turn a substance that cannot be assimilated by green plants into one that can. But they also help to make other substances available. Sulfur, for example, is a constituent of some proteins essential to living things, but it too can be absorbed by plants only in soluble forms, some of which are not naturally present in soil. Bacteria play a major role in decomposing dead plants and animal remains and releasing soluble sulfur compounds. One of the substances that the bacteria produce in this process is hydrogen sulfide gas—giving rotting materials their distinctive smell of bad eggs.

Almost all the free-living microorganisms that we have discussed so far need to find their food ready-made. Exceptions are the blue-green algae and the true algae. True algae are green plants, and as such are on the other side of the biological fence from microbes, which need to hunt and compete for their food. With the sugar that they manufacture by photosynthesis, together with small amounts of nitrogen, sulfur, and other vital elements, they can undertake the

complex chemistry involved in creating the substances required for growth. Once incorporated into green plants, these substances are available to any creature that eats them.

Over half the new plant material created each year is produced by land plants. But the remainder—in specific terms about 50,000 million tons—is produced by water-dwelling green algae.

Green algae live mainly in coastal waters and estuaries—the "nurseries of the sea"—and in inland lakes and ponds. They need water rich in nutrients to survive. Some open-ocean areas also support algal populations, however, especially off the coasts of California and Peru, where winds and currents cause the up-welling of deep ocean water, bringing nutrients to the surface.

Green algae drifting in the sea are called *phytoplankton*—which means plant plankton. The mass of living organisms, plant and animal, that simply float at or near the surface and are carried about by the water's movements are known collectively as the *plankton*. Most phytoplankton live near enough to the surface for sunshine to reach them, so that they can photosynthesize. The phytoplankton have been called the "pastures of the sea," and they are extremely lush pastures. They are eaten by their larger

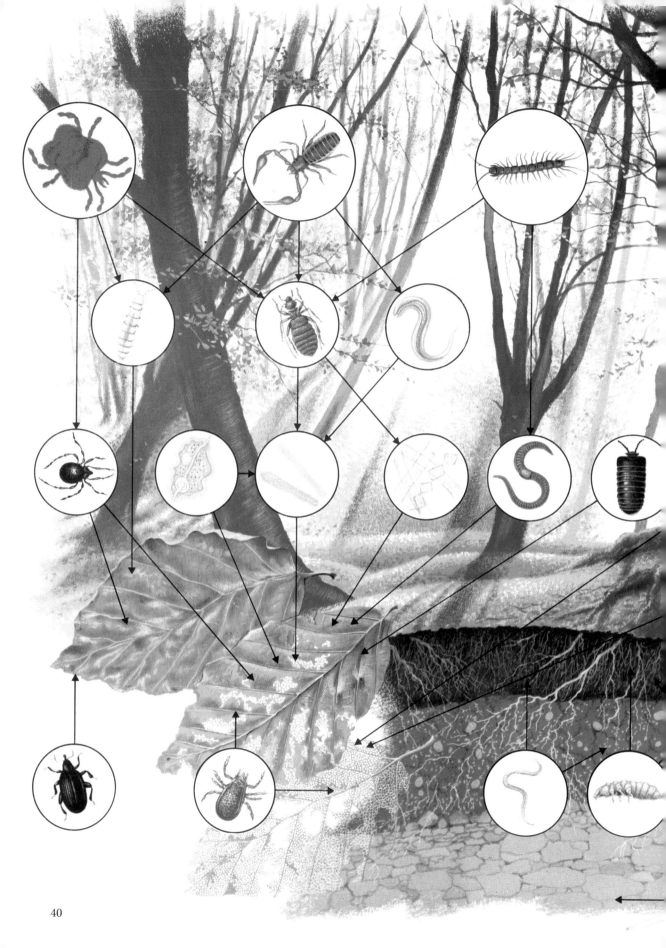

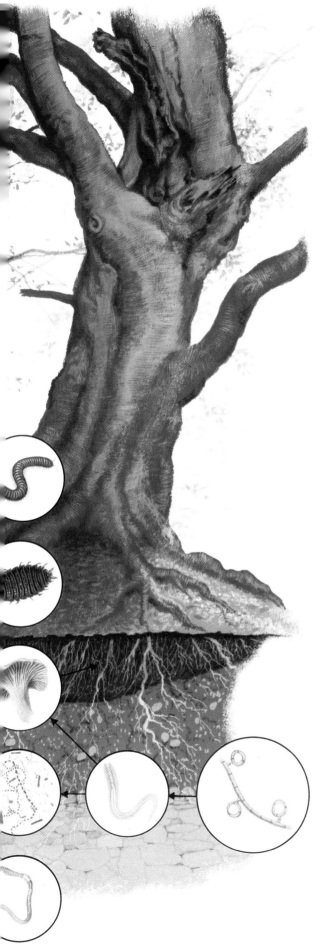

The Invisible World of a Woodland Floor

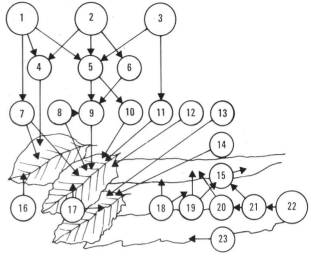

1 Predatory mite	13 Millipede
2 Pseudoscorpion	14 Sowbug
3 Centipede	(woodlouse)
4 Springtail	15 Fungi
5 Psocid (booklouse)	16 Weevil
6 Nematode	17 Mite
7 Mite	18 Earthworm
8 Protozoa	19 Springtail
9 Bacteria	20 Bacteria
10 Algae	21 Nematode
11 Earthworm	22 Predatory fungus
12 Pillbug (woodlouse)	23 Earthworm

A host of hungry creatures are involved in decomposing the leaves that fall onto a woodland floor: many of them are invisible microorganisms, others the tiniest of insects, some (such as the earthworms) big enough to be easily visible. But we are seldom aware even of those we can see, because their habitat is hidden in the litter layer or deeper. As indicated by the arrows, various food chains begin with the decaying leaf, which, as it gradually decomposes, sinks down through three layers of soil (whose relative depths are not drawn to scale in this picture): a dark upper layer of humus, which is associated with tree roots; a second, lighter zone that includes both organic material and earth; and the lightest level, composed almost entirely of mineral soil. The system pictured here is based on what happens to beech leaves, but it is fairly typical for any litter breakdowns in woodland areas in the temperate zone.

animal neighbors in the plankton mass—the so-called *zooplankton*—and by other animals, including whales.

Just as vegetation on land changes with the seasons, so the drifting life of the sea in temperate regions alters with the succession of winter, spring, summer, and autumn. In the dark days of winter, there is little light for photosynthesis, and so the phytoplankton, unable to manufacture food for themselves, begin to dwindle in number. The small animals that make up the zooplankton are thus deprived of their natural food, and they too die away. The millions of tiny dead bodies replenish the water with vital nutrients, almost as if the sea were being manured ready for spring.

When spring comes, the bright sunshine stimulates the growth of the algae, and this abundance of food allows the zooplankton to grow and reproduce. Within the space of a few weeks, the planktonic population may have multiplied 10,000 times over. But the warmth that brings on the spring outburst of marine life also has another interesting effect; it heats the surface layers of the water, which become less dense than the lower, colder layers. The plankton in the warm surface water grow and multiply until, having used up all the available nutrients, vast numbers of them die. The dead bodies sink into the cold, lower layers, and so the surviving planktonic population is deprived of the valuable products of their decay.

In this magnified color photograph of diatoms and blue-green algae, the two kinds of organisms are readily distinguishable; naviculoid diatoms are boat-shaped, whereas Oscillatoria blue-green algae consist of thin filaments, either in individual strands or matted together into bundles.

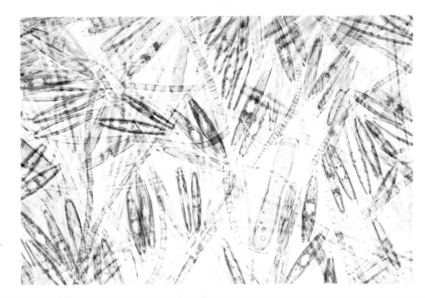

The obvious fertility of the Japanese rice farm below owes much to the micro-organisms that inhabit its watery soil, for the soluble nitrates without which plants cannot survive are produced from gaseous nitrogen by the activities of free-living microbes, particularly the blue-green algae that abound in the waters of Asian paddy fields.

In the autumn, when there is no hot sunshine to heat the water, the surface layers cool off again, and the autumn gales and winds churn the upper and lower layers together. Once more, the temporarily lost nutrients become available to the planktonic community. The tiny creatures respond with an autumnal outburst of life—less spectacular than that of the spring, but enough to enable the plankton to survive the rigors of the winter.

The algae floating in the water are at the mercy of the elements, nourished by whatever nutrients come their way, and are likely at any time to be devoured by the fish and mammals for which the plankton provide a perpetual dinner table. Life is perhaps a little easier for the microbes living on the seabed or at the bottom of a pond. If you look very hard at the bottom of a pond or stream, you are likely to catch a glimpse of the dark brown, fuzzy material that clings to the stones and other surfaces, which is made up of a mixed population of algae, bacteria, and fungi.

Free-living microorganisms, then, have greatly

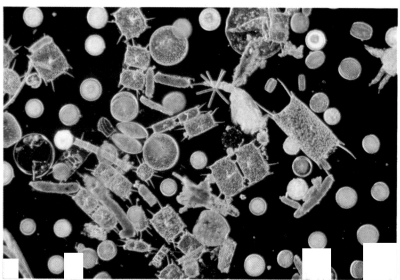

Most of the sea's plant life is found in the phytoplankton, which is composed of minute single-celled plants of many shapes and sizes. Left: various species of diatom, along with animal feces (the round pellets) and one copepod (a tiny crustacean member of the zooplankton). The distinguishing feature of a diatom, whatever its shape, is the hard cell wall that surrounds it like a box. Above: a ship sails through a swarm of Noctiluca scintillans—dinoflagellates that form pinkish drifts at the surface of calm summer seas. Near right: a close-up of a few of these densely packed creatures, which are luminescent at night when agitated by a passing ship. Far right: another member of the dinoflagellates. Most dinoflagellates have two flagella, extending from the center of the cell.

influenced the patterns of development of life in many ways. They have also influenced the development of the nonliving physical world. And their influence here is sometimes beneficial, but often harmful, to man.

Certain bacteria, for example, are responsible for the formation of the foul-smelling black mud found on the seabed and in coastal areas, where their life processes create a compound of sulfur and iron that gives the mud its distinctive color and appearance. Apart from its odor, the black mud is comparatively harmless. But the same kind of bacteria whose activities form the mud can also be the corrosive agents that attack iron and steel pipes buried either in the seabed or in the soil. These pipes are open to attack from rusting in any case, but the bacteria help matters along considerably. In the Netherlands, water pipes often have to be laid in land that has been reclaimed from the sea, and they are coated with asphalt to give protection. Nevertheless, the pipes can become so corroded in a year or two that the iron can be cut with a knife as though it were butter. Ordinary rusting without bac-

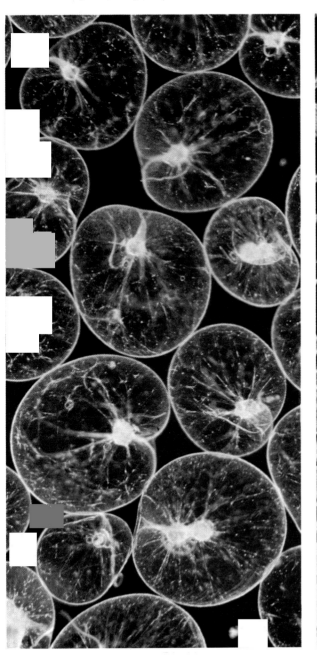

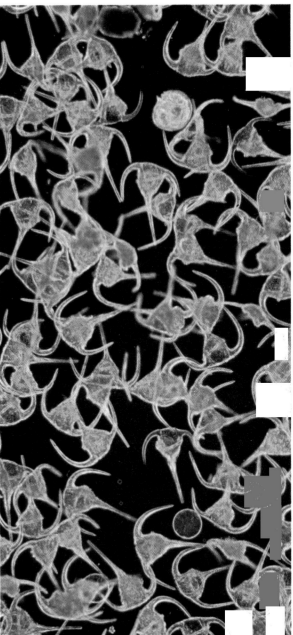

This gigantic snail-like bowl, which lies near the Mexico City Airport, is actually called "the snail" (El Caracol). It gets its fascinating succession of colors from the microorganisms that live in the salt water that flows through it. The bowl, two miles in diameter, was built by a company that manufactures soda and salt. Brine fed into the spiral flows slowly down the gradient until it reaches the center—a distance of 20 miles in all. From start to finish, the sluggish process takes 6 months, during which time water evaporates and the salt content of the brine becomes more and more concentrated. Meanwhile, the algae and bacteria in the solution change the color of the bowl as its contents get closer to the middle.

47

terial assistance could not do so swift a job of destruction.

On the other hand, it seems likely that microorganisms played a partial but significant role in the formation of the fossil fuels—peat, coal, and oil—that we prize so highly. What probably happened, millions of years ago, was that huge amounts of partly decayed vegetable matter became embedded in the mud at the bottom of shallow marshes and lakes. Through the course of time, this vegetation became covered with layers of sand and rock. But bacteria are very efficient at decomposing dead organic remains;

why, then, should this great mass of vegetation have remained undecomposed for the natural geological processes of compression to turn it into fossil fuels?

The answer seems to be that the vegetation was probably waterlogged, and so it is unlikely that there was sufficient oxygen available for bacterial decomposition. The only bacteria that could go to work on the vegetation in that case would have been those that did not require oxygen for life. Such bacteria, we know, produce acids while breaking down organic matter— acids that are lethal to the very bacteria that

Peat, coal, and oil—the compressed vegetation from which we get most of our energy—became fossil fuels partly because of microbial action. Instead of being decomposed, the waterlogged plant life that we now burn was only partly decayed, probably by acid-producing bacteria whose own acid seems to have killed them before they could finish the job. Right: turf cutting in Ireland, where peat is widely used. Although peat—a burnable type of turf—is easier to reach than coal or oil, it is far less energy-productive. Below: off-shore drilling for oil in Alaska.

produce them. So decomposition would have ceased at the stage of acid production, leaving the partly decayed vegetation to be compressed and turned into peat, coal, or oil.

It is an interesting fact that the micro-organisms that played a role in the formation of coal and oil now play a role in helping man to prospect for these substances. Where there are deposits of coal or oil, a number of gases such at methane, ethane, and propane may seep to the surface and provide nutrients for certain kinds of microorganism that can grow in these gases in the absence of oxygen. Wherever such bacteria seem to be thriving—and they can be discovered through laboratory analysis of the soil—there is a good chance that a fossil-fuel deposit will be found nearby.

The invisible decomposers are still at work forming peat in bogs and marshes. A frequent by-product of this bacterial activity is marsh

49

gas, or methane. It can be seen bubbling from peat bogs, where it sometimes ignites spontaneously, giving rise at night to the will-o'-the-wisp that used to be blamed for luring unwary travelers off the safe path and into the deadly marshes. In modern times, methane has proved to be invaluable to mankind, for great pockets of it have been discovered throughout the world, and these are tapped to provide heat and power for domestic use and for industry.

We have concerned ourselves up to this point with free-living microorganisms at work in the soil and at home in the water. What about the atmosphere, the region in the biosphere that we have not yet mentioned? The answer is that for most microorganisms the air is a medium of transmission rather than a habitat. It is full of

Right: shallow standing waters are often clogged with living material (the periphyton) built up chiefly from algae and containing well over 100 different representatives of microorganic plant and animal life. Among them may sometimes be found the strange, primitive monster pictured above. This tardigrade (or "water bear"), though not technically a microbe, is nonetheless too small to be easily seen with the naked eye; a scanning electron micrograph has magnified it to 150 times its actual size. One remarkable characteristic of the tardigrades is their ability to survive very extensive periods of drought. They have been known to return to life after as much as seven years of virtual nonexistence in a shriveled state.

living organisms, but most of them are in their resistant spore form—the well-protected packages that germinate and produce growing organisms only when they alight on a suitably life-supporting surface.

Measurements made not long ago in one of the world's biggest cities, London, indicate that there are as many as 14 living spores in each cubic foot of air outdoors. Indoors, the total may be very much higher, and up to 1000 spores per cubic foot have been recorded. The difference in the numbers of microorganisms in a cubic foot of outdoor air compared with a cubic foot of indoor air may seem remarkable; in fact, however, most of the indoor organisms come from the human respiratory system. Up to 100,000 bacteria may be expelled in a single sneeze, and so it is perhaps remarkable that the indoor figure is not even higher.

Fungal spores are the most common of the microflora in the air, but there are also bacterial cells and spores, virus particles, and occasional algal cells. At some seasons there will certainly be pollen grains from flowering plants, too. It is largely the pollen grains that cause hay fever, but certain fungal spores also have unpleasant effects on people who are allergic to them. Farmer's lung, a complaint sometimes suffered by farm workers, is the result of an allergic response to chemical substances present in the airborne spores of fungi that live on hay.

Fungi in general have developed a wide range

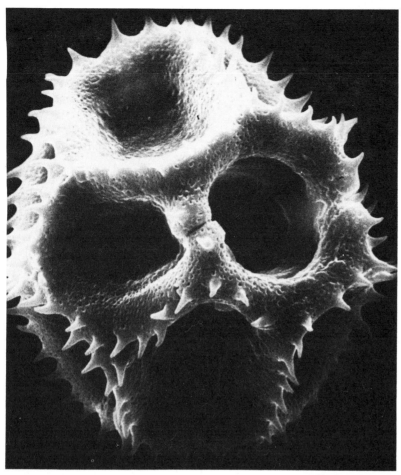

The air is less a habitat for micro-organisms than a medium of transmission, and so its flora consists mainly of pollen grains and fungal and bacterial spores for dispersal and reproduction. This dandelion pollen grain (left), magnified to 3000 times its true size, is a typical example of the kind of airborne pollen that bedevils hay-fever sufferers. but some people are also allergic to fungal spores. Below left: a water droplet lands on the sporophore within the star-shaped outer case of an earthstar fungus, inducing it to expel a cloud of spores for the wind to carry away. A rather more powerful triggering instrument than the drop of water is the combine pictured below. If there is any fungal rust in this American wheat field, spore clouds liberated into the air by the combine may infect other wheat fields hundreds of miles away.

of mechanisms to exploit the air as a means of spore dispersal. Some, such as the mushrooms and toadstools, erect large fleshy structures from which spores are launched into the atmosphere and carried away in the air. Simpler fungi erect only a single threadlike stalk with a ball of spores at the end. In more complex varieties, spores may be ejected like tiny projectiles.

Microbial spores can be carried long distances by wind. Whenever crops are attacked by fungi, there is almost certain to be a vast production of fungal spores. Fungal rust and mildew, in particular, give off great clouds of spores, which may travel a very long way. In America, the fungal disease wheat rust travels north from Mexico and infects crops as far away as the Canadian prairies. In northern Europe, wheat can be infected by rust spores carried by wind from Portugal or Algeria.

Some species of bacteria, if their growth is threatened by the exhaustion of an essential nutrient or by some other sort of harsh condition, form endospores. These can remain dormant for many years, whether in the soil, in water, or in air, but they can germinate to produce normal cells in a matter of minutes. We shall see in Chapter 5 how airborne spores can spread fungal and bacterial diseases.

And so in their quest for survival, in their never-ending battle against the elements and competing organisms for the raw materials of life, free-living microorganisms have changed, and are still changing, the face of the earth. Indeed, they profoundly influence all aspects of life on this planet, and we see their effects everywhere, although they themselves are invisible. In the next few chapters we shall look at the life styles of those microorganisms that are not free-living but that depend on other living creatures for their food and housing.

Plants and Microbes

Two can live as cheaply as one, they say: and for many plants and animals some sort of close relationship has become a way of life and a hedge against the possibility of extinction. The diversity of nature gives amazing scope for different types of association between living things: animal with animal, plant with plant, animal with plant—and microorganisms with every kind of organism you can think of. Such associations may provide protection against the elements and may vastly improve the partners' chances· of having an adequate food supply.

In this chapter we shall look at associations between microorganisms and plants, ranging from the very loose to the very intimate. Mutually helpful associations of plant and microbe are sometimes helpful to man, for on some of these depends the success of important food crops. And harmful associations can hurt us by damaging our crops, occasionally changing the course of history as they do so.

The fungus that causes potato blight, for example, has had an impact not only on the history of plant disease, but on the history of the world in general. When this fungus ravaged the Irish potato crop in 1845 and in the years following, the consequent widespread famine in Ireland resulted in mass migrations to England and America. It was only later that scientists discovered that the disease was caused by a fungus—a discovery that led to an entirely new understanding of the importance of fungi in plant disease.

But although the question of whether an association is harmful or beneficial to man may be uppermost in the mind of the farmer or the politician (who has to vote the necessary money for controlling the microorganisms that destroy food crops), the ecologist examines each case from a different standpoint. He wants to understand the relationship between different forms

Clover growing in a field. The ability of leguminous plants such as clover to improve soil and secure heavier crops has been known to farmers for 2000 years. We know now that nodules on their roots contain special bacteria capable of turning atmospheric nitrogen into soil-enriching compounds.

54

macabre effect on at least one group of human beings. All of us have a certain amount of radioactivity in our bodies as a result of the testing of atomic weapons in the atmosphere, but the Eskimos have unusually high levels of the dangerous radioactive chemicals cesium 137 and strontium 90 in their bones. The reason is that in the tundra regions rainwater with radioactive fallout has been absorbed by the resident lichens—chiefly reindeer moss and Iceland moss (which are called "moss," but are lichens). These "mosses" are the chief source of food for the reindeer, which in turn are eaten by Eskimos. And so radioactive substances pass through the food chain to the human beings.

Another remarkable thing about the marriage of alga and fungus that forms lichen is its slow growth, along with exceptional durability. Most mature lichens grow only one millimeter or less each year. The age of lichens growing on objects of known age—tombstones, for instance—can

be deduced, and it seems they can live for 200 years or more. Naturalists have found Arctic species up to 4500 years old. Indeed, some lichens grow so slowly that geologists use them to estimate the age of glacial deposits. Obviously, for the association to persist for such a long time, the natural balance between the two partners has to be an extremely fine one. Yet it does not take much to upset this balance. It is a severely limited supply of nutrients that apparently causes an alga and a fungus to join forces; if adequately nourished, each of them can survive on its own. Thus, if a lichen is removed from its natural home and given plenty of food and water in a laboratory, the association may break down spontaneously. Either the fungus destroys the alga or the alga overgrows the fungus.

Just as it requires a fine balance for the two microorganisms to sustain their intimate relationship, so the lichen's method of reproduction is a very delicate operation. Some

Lichen (below) is a dual organism, part fungus part alga, both of which are dependent on each other. Often brilliantly colored, as shown on the rocks pictured opposite, lichen are among the first plants to colonize bare inhospitable ground.

Potato Blight

of life, and so he wants to know not only how the microorganism affects the plant, but how the plant affects the microorganism.

Let us start, then, by looking at a remarkable example of two microbial plants, an alga and a fungus, that live together for their mutual benefit. They have become so adapted to their interdependent life style that many people think the result is a single plant. We call this familiar partnership a *lichen*. About 18,000 different species of lichen have been identified, and they show a wide variety of shapes and colors. What you see and recognize as lichen is certainly visible, but we should remember that it is made up of many invisible single-celled components. And the two partners are so tightly bound together that it is impossible to distinguish them as separate organisms without a powerful microscope. Indeed, botanists began to realize that a lichen is a microbial cooperative only a little over a century ago. Before then, when they examined these symbiotic creatures through the microscope, they believed that the green algal cells in the lichen were its reproductive organs.

Typically, a lichen consists of a layer of algal cells embedded in a layer of fungal tissue. Most fungi are composed of a mass of threadlike filaments, and in lichens these filaments are wound tightly together to form the lichen proper, whereas the algal cells lie in a thin layer just below the surface. It is clear that the fungi get their nourishment from the photosynthetic green algae by means of special feeding tubes, which penetrate the algal cells. Although the algae may make up only 5 or 10 per cent of the weight of the entire lichen, they can supply both their own food needs and those of the fungi; in fact, scientists have shown that about half of all the food the alga makes goes to the fungus.

What does the alga get in return for this openhandedness? Some scientists believe that the fungus protects the alga from adverse conditions, especially shortage of water, and also

This illustration shows various stages of potato blight, a fungus related to some of the mildews, and water and bread molds. 1. A potato in the first stages of attack. 2. The fungus spreads into the inner tissues. 3. Fungus growing in a spiral around a small "ash-leaved" potato. In 4, 5, and 7, fungal hyphae can be seen threading through potato cells. 6. The blight has darkened cells in the stem, and threads through leaf tissues (8 and 9) to send up spore shoots through the leaf stomata.

provides a firm base where the alga can grow without much danger of erosion by rain or wind or of an overdose of sunlight, which can kill free-living algae. Others think that the alga gets no benefit at all from the association—in other words, that the fungus lives off the alga without doing it any harm. Still others feel fairly sure that both organisms derive benefits, but they admit they do not yet know what the association does for the alga.

Whatever the nature of the relationship, it is certainly finely balanced and effective, for lichens frequently grow in areas and conditions that few other living things could tolerate (and that includes algae or fungi living on their own). The photosynthetic partner in some lichens is the blue-green alga genus *Nostoc* (which, you may remember, is not a true alga at all but rather akin to a bacterium in structure). Because *Nostoc* can convert atmospheric nitrogen into soluble compounds, a lichen that combines a species of *Nostoc* with a fungus is extraordinarily self-sufficient. It can manufacture its own food, obtain its own nitrogen, resist desiccation, and absorb vital minerals from unyielding surfaces.

This ability to absorb minerals, however, is a hazard as well as a blessing. Lichens are resistant to direct sunlight, drought, heat, and cold, but they cannot tolerate the polluted atmosphere of cities, or any kind of industrial pollution. The apparent reason for this is that the lichens extract minerals and other substances from rainwater; in polluted areas the rain may contain high concentrations of poisonous substances, and the lichens extract these as readily as they absorb useful minerals. Because the lichens have no means of getting rid of the poisons, they are eventually killed off.

In Europe, where lichen growth is used as an indicator of atmospheric pollution, it has been shown that the number of lichen species decreases toward the center of a city. For example, 10 miles from Newcastle-upon-Tyne, an industrial city in northern England, over 50 different species of lichen can be found flourishing; five miles from the city center, fewer than 20 species can tolerate the polluted air; and virtually none are to be found in the center itself. If you see lichen on tree trunks close to a factory, you can justifiably guess that it belongs to one of the very few species resistant to pollutants.

The ability of lichens to absorb and concentrate chemicals from rainwater has had a macabre effect on at least one group of human beings. All of us have a certain amount of radioactivity in our bodies as a result of the testing of atomic weapons in the atmosphere, but the Eskimos have unusually high levels of the dangerous radioactive chemicals cesium 137 and strontium 90 in their bones. The reason is that in the tundra regions rainwater with radioactive fallout has been absorbed by the resident lichens—chiefly reindeer moss and Iceland moss (which are called "moss," but are lichens). These "mosses" are the chief source of food for the reindeer, which in turn are eaten by Eskimos. And so radioactive substances pass through the food chain to the human beings.

Another remarkable thing about the marriage of alga and fungus that forms lichen is its slow growth, along with exceptional durability. Most mature lichens grow only one millimeter or less each year. The age of lichens growing on objects of known age—tombstones, for instance—can be deduced, and it seems they can live for 200 years or more. Naturalists have found Arctic species up to 4500 years old. Indeed, some lichens grow so slowly that geologists use them to estimate the age of glacial deposits. Obviously, for the association to persist for such a long time, the natural balance between the two partners has to be an extremely fine one. Yet it does not take much to upset this balance. It is a severely limited supply of nutrients that apparently causes an alga and a fungus to join forces; if adequately nourished, each of them can survive on its own. Thus, if a lichen is removed from its natural home and given plenty of food and water in a laboratory, the association may break down spontaneously. Either the fungus destroys the alga or the alga overgrows the fungus.

Just as it requires a fine balance for the two microorganisms to sustain their intimate relationship, so the lichen's method of reproduction is a very delicate operation. Some

Lichen (below) is a dual organism, part fungus part alga, both of which are dependent on each other. Often brilliantly colored, as shown on the rocks pictured opposite, lichen are among the first plants to colonize bare inhospitable ground.

lichens—for example, *Xanthoria parietina,* an orange-yellow lichen that flourishes on the rocks by the seashore—have adopted a rather risky technique: the fungus produces dispersal spores, which it shoots out into the atmosphere to be carried away by the wind, and the lichen can be formed again only if the fungal spores germinate alongside cells of the algal partner (in this case a species of *Trebouxia*). If there are plenty of organic nutrients available, any spore can of course produce a healthy fungus on its own; but if nutrients are in poor supply, the fungus will not survive without the help of its algal partner. Other lichens take less risk by producing special dispersal packages consisting of a few algal cells wrapped inside a few fine threads of fungus. These packages are blown away to germinate as new lichens of the same type.

Marriages of the kind that produce lichens are not common in nature. Most microbes that live in association with larger plants enjoy a more casual relationship with their green partners—a relationship that is often so casual, in fact, that its nature can only be guessed at. What is quite clear is that the roots and leaves of green plants usually carry large numbers of microorganisms on their surfaces, and that the soil around the roots is also rich in microorganisms. The area where the roots meet the soil is called the *rhizosphere;* and if you dig up a plant and examine the rhizosphere, you will almost certainly find that its color is slightly different from that of the surrounding earth. This is because microorganisms are at work in the immediate vicinity of the roots.

Scientists have devised ways of looking at plant roots while they are still alive in the soil. Large concentrations of microbes can be seen around the growing root. Soil bacteria evidently cluster in large clumps on the rootlets, even forming fully enveloping sheaths around them, and hordes of bacteria swim in the thin layer of water that surrounds the roots. The fine threads of various species of fungus can be seen winding through the network of roots and rootlets, sometimes putting forth an exploratory thread of living fungus to penetrate the outer tissues of the root. With all this readily available food, it is hardly surprising that predatory protozoans and tiny nematode worms are abundant, feeding on the bacteria and the fungi.

What benefit do the bacteria and fungi draw from their association with plant roots? Chiefly

nutrients, for roots are not watertight and are bound to leak out such substances as sugars, amino acids (the basic components of protein), vitamins, and other substances that microorganisms can use for growth. Some species of *Bacillus* bacteria secrete chemical substances, rather like powerful household detergents, that actually increase the leakiness of plant roots. The large plant, on the other hand, seems to get very little from such loose associations, although it is possible that the presence of the organisms of the rhizosphere in some way helps the plant to absorb chemicals from the soil.

Sometimes the microorganisms around its roots can positively harm a plant. One group of bacteria get their energy through a chemical reaction involving the element manganese. Healthy oat crops need manganese; and if their rhizosphere is overburdened with manganese-using bacteria, the resultant deprivation gives the oats what is known as "gray-speck disease." The cure is to suffuse the soil with a chemical that poisons the bacteria without hurting the oat crop.

The aerial parts of plants—stems and leaves—also have casual microbial associates. The problems that these microorganisms must solve in order to maintain such above-ground relationships are quite different from those in the rhizosphere. The greatest problem is desiccation. It is not surprising, therefore, that most plants with extensive microbial populations on the leaves are tropical in origin. Because of the high humidity of most tropical regions, the aerial parts of tropical plants are often coated with a fine film of moisture, which encourages the growth of microorganisms. A rubber tree, for example, may harbor over 65 million microorganisms on each square inch of its leaf surface. And they are well fed, too. The waxy cuticle on tropical plants is thinner than that on temperate species, for water loss is much less of a problem, and so various leaf constituents ooze out onto the surface and become available to the trespassers. Flowers that produce sugary nectar to attract the insects for pollination are also ideal sources of food for microorganisms.

The invisible creatures that live on leaves and stems do little harm, even though some of the bacteria produce gums or slime to help themselves adhere to the leaves during heavy rainfall. But there is at least one exception to this general rule. When aphids attack a rosebush,

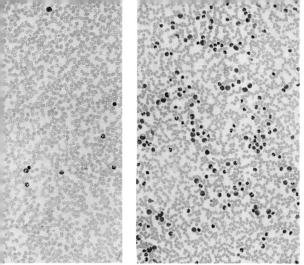

Photomicrographs of blood taken from a leukemia—blood cancer—sufferer (above right) compared with normal blood (above left). Scientists think that strontium 90 might be a possible cause of the disease. Reindeer moss (right), which absorbs and concentrates minerals from rainwater, contains a high proportion of strontium 90. The moss, which is in fact a lichen despite its name, is eaten by reindeer (below), a principal, and probably dangerous, food source of the Eskimos.

How Microbes and Plants can Benefit Each Other

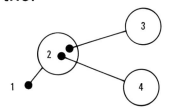

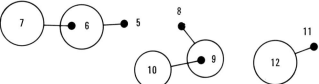

Lichen – alga/fungus association
1 Lichen growing on bark of birch tree.
2 Enlarged cross section through lichen.
3 Algal cells.
4 Fungal hyphae.

A lichen is a symbiotic association between an alga and a fungus. The algal cells are the photosynthetic components of the lichen. These are embedded in a mass of fungal tissue, which obtains its food from the algal cells and, in return, provides protection for the thin algal layer.

Ectotrophic (external) mycorrhiza – root/fungus association
5 Hyphae of fly agaric fungus surrounding roots of birch tree.
6 Enlarged portion of mycorrhizal birch tree roots.
7 Cross section through mycorrhizal roots showing the fungal sheath as a dark outer band.

A mycorrhiza is a symbiotic association between the roots of a higher green plant and a fungus. An ectotrophic mycorrhiza is one in which the fungus forms a sheath around the outside of the root. The fungus gets all the sugar it needs from its host and the green plant obtains mineral salts from the fungus.

Root nodule of legume – root/bacterium association
8 Root system of clover showing nodules, which contain bacteria.
9 Enlarged view of clover root system.
10 *Rhizobium* bacteria from nodules of clover root.

Root nodules are formed as a result of a specific symbiotic association between a leguminous plant and bacteria of the genus *Rhizobium.* The bacteria collaborate with the plant in the process of converting gaseous nitrogen into nitrogen compounds that both the plant and the bacteria need for nourishment.

Endotrophic (internal) mycorrhiza – root/fungus association
11 Root system of orchid.
12 Longitudinal section through orchid mycorrhiza showing fungal hyphae within root cells.

An endotrophic mycorrhiza is one in which the fungus actually penetrates the tissues of the root. The relationship between the two partners is not fully known but it seems that the green plants involved do need the fungi for successful growth.

they pierce the leaves with their sharp mouth-parts in order to get at the sap. As they feed, they deposit droplets of sticky honeydew on the leaf surface. These droplets are rapidly colonized by fungi, and the growth of these fungi, together with the formation of fungal reproductive spores, forms a dense, sooty-black coating on the leaf surface. This undermines the capacity of the rosebush to manufacture its food, for the fungal coating not only reduces the amount of light that reaches the photosynthetic tissue of the leaf but also blocks the stomata—the pores through which carbon dioxide reaches these tissues.

Even this last relationship is a highly casual one, however, for although the rosebush is a host to the fungus, it is the honeydew, not the plant, that nurtures the microorganisms.

Now let us look at examples of much more specific relationships between green plants and microorganisms—associations, first of all, that truly benefit each partner in the arrange-ment. The most important such association—to man, at any rate—is found in peas, beans, and other leguminous plants that have formed a remarkable alliance with bacteria of the genus *Rhizobium*. So intimate and specific is this relationship that the plant forms special lumpy structures, or nodules, on its roots to house its bacterial partner. You can see these clearly if you pull up a legume and wash the roots.

Such a sophisticated arrangement must be based on peculiarly valuable advantages to be had from the association. The key to the matter is the fact that the *Rhizobium* bacteria col-laborate with the plant in the act of converting gaseous nitrogen into nitrogen compounds (a process called *nitrogen fixation*) that both the plant and the microorganism need for nourish-ment. Unlike certain free-living nitrogen-fixing bacteria or the blue-green nitrogen-fixing alga that forms part of several types of lichen, neither the *Rhizobium* bacteria nor the leguminous

Below: runner bean plant awaiting harvesting. They belong to an important group of plants called legumes. Below right: swellings, or nodules, which are packed with bacteria, grow on the roots. The bacteria are fed by the plant and in return they turn atmospheric nitrogen into compounds that can be used by the plant.

plants in whose root nodules they live can fix nitrogen by themselves. They can do it only in close partnership with each other.

Actually, both the bacterium and the plant can survive without each other if each is supplied with its own source of absorbable nitrogen, and so the relationship is in no way obligatory. (In fact, if we did not know that the root nodules fix nitrogen, we might easily assume that the bacterium is harmful to the plant, because the nodules look like abnormal tumors.) But although the two organisms are not absolutely necessary to each other, they do much better together than apart. In nitrogen-deficient soils, for example, legumes with root nodules grow far faster than those without the nodules.

The inside of the mature nitrogen-fixing nodule in which the bacteria live is bright red in color because it contains a protein that is like hemoglobin, the iron-containing protein that gives red blood its color. Neither the plant nor the microorganism alone is responsible for the formation of this red pigment; it is formed as a result of cooperation.

Exactly how the plant and the bacteria work together to fix nitrogen remains a mystery in spite of extensive scientific study, nor is it known why peas and beans should be so especially favored. Some scientists point out, however, that many leguminous plants are tropical in origin, and their ancestral home was the tropical rain forest, where the soils had been washed virtually free of nutrients by the ceaseless rainfall. Thus, they would have had to find a different way to acquire such nutrients.

Although we do not yet know how they work together, we do know how the plant gets its colony of bacteria and forms its root nodules. Like those of all land plants, the roots of leguminous species allow some nutrients to pass into the surrounding soil, and this stimulates the growth of the bacteria in the rhizosphere. A special layer gradually develops around the outside of the leguminous root, thus preventing the nutrients from draining away into the soil. As the layer develops, the rhizosphere bacteria become concentrated in an ever-growing band. Within this enclosed space, the growth of bacteria of the *Rhizobium* type is favored, but the other microorganisms die off. The *Rhizobium* bacteria grow and multiply, infecting the root through the root hairs (hairlike projections

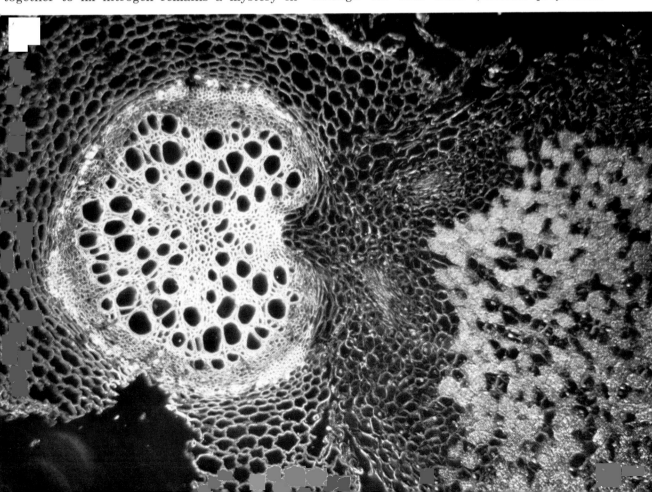

from the root surface, which play an important part in water and mineral salt absorption).

Some of the normally rod-shaped bacteria become transformed into spherical "swarmer cells" covered with whiplike flagellae for swimming; and they wriggle their way through the layer surrounding the root, and so enter the plant's root hairs. What seems to happen is that *Rhizobium* produces a chemical substance, probably a hormone, that affects the root hairs of leguminous plants in such a way as to "soften" them for the invasion.

Once inside a root hair, the swarmer cells proliferate and grow, forming a so-called "infection thread," which leads down the root hair to the body of its cell. There are always a number of especially receptive cells in the roots of these plants, and if one of these is infected by the swarmer cells, it begins to divide and form a nodule. Eventually, any such nodule becomes filled with a new form of *Rhizobium,* known as *bacteroids,* which are swollen and often branched.

Leguminous root nodules confer three separate sets of benefits—first, on the plant, which gains a steady source of nitrogen in a readily usable form; secondly, on the bacteria, which gain shelter and an easy supply of sugars; thirdly, on humanity. Long before he understood the biology and biochemistry of nitrogen fixation, man was making use of the nitrogen-fixing properties of leguminous crops to maintain the fertility of his fields. The ability of plants such as vetch and lucerne (or alfalfa) to enrich soil was known in biblical times. It formed the basis of the crop-rotation schemes developed during the Middle Ages, when farmers learned to grow clover and other legumes and to plow them back into the soil before sowing the main crop.

Nodules fix very large amounts of nitrogen. A healthy lucerne nodule can more than double its own nitrogen content in a day. Worldwide, about 1000 million tons of nitrogen are fixed annually by living organisms, and most of this comes from leguminous plants. New Zealanders, for example, rarely add nitrogen fertilizers to their soil. Instead, they grow a lot of clover, and it has been estimated that the bacteria-filled nodules in such clover-planted soil fix as much as 500 pounds per acre of atmospheric nitrogen every year. Even though the equivalent figure for nitrogen fixation by root nodules in most areas is only a little more than half as much, it is still true that the leguminous plant-

Rhizobium partnership ordinarily produces an annual amount of useful nitrogen compounds equal to a field treatment of three quarters of a ton of the best nitrogen fertilizer.

A few other types of plant also have root nodules containing nitrogen-fixing bacteria. Among them are the sea buckthorn and the bog myrtle. Some tropical plants have *leaf* nodules, which contain nitrogen-fixing bacteria of a different genus from *Rhizobium*. There are also some similar, but less clearly defined, nitrogen-fixing associations, such as that between one kind of water fern and the blue-green alga *Anabaena*. The leaves of the fern have small mucilage-filled chambers that contain these microscopic algae, but the relationship is less obviously a mutually dependent one than the legume–*Rhizobium* association. *Anabaena* seems

Below right: a grain of soil (magnified 640 times) containing some of the vast population of soil microorganisms which, by breaking down dead plants and animals, release substances essential to plant life. After intensive crop-growing, the soil microorganisms need time to build up fresh supplies of nutrients. Early farmers knew only that by periodically resting their fields they could improve crop yields. Top right: the three strip fields in this plan of a typical European feudal village were worked in yearly rotation—the strips worked by one villager are marked in red. The fields are colored to indicate plowing sequence: yellow and brown are spring and fall plowing, pale yellow is fallow, or resting. Below: medieval peasant farmers in their fields.

able to fix nitrogen equally well whether inside the host plant or outside. Then, too, there is a nitrogen-fixing bacterium commonly found on the leaves of tropical plants, but we do not yet know how interdependent the two organisms are. It may be that this bacterium represents a halfway stage between the free-living style of life and the intimate, specialized partnership.

So far we have concentrated chiefly on the associations between bacteria and plant roots. Fungi and roots also live together, and their associations are no less binding and significant. The name for a symbiotic association of fungi and the roots of large green plants is *mycorrhiza* (which means literally "root fungus"). It seems likely that the roots of a high proportion of land plants share their subterranean lives with one fungus or another. In a forest, for example, almost every tree will have a fungal partner wrapped around its roots. In forests of conifer, beech, or oak trees, the fungus forms a sheath around the roots. Much more common, however, is the kind of mycorrhiza in which the fungus actually penetrates the roots, as happens with

orchids. Yet we know a good deal more about the relationship between the forest trees and their external fungal associates than we do about the more common ingrowing root fungi.

Three soil conditions must be met before mycorrhizal fungi will develop readily on tree roots: the soil must be well-ventilated, contain an abundance of decaying plant matter, and be comparatively poor in inorganic plant nutrients. These conditions are relatively common in soils that support plant life, and it is not surprising that so many plants have their associated mycorrhizal fungi. The benefits to the partners are obvious: the fungus gets from its host all the sugar it needs for growth, and the tree gets a greater share of whatever mineral salts are to be had from the soil, for fungi are very good at accumulating such substances.

In soils that are poorly supplied with inorganic nutrients, trees with mycorrhiza thrive, whereas those that are uninfected do not. The mutual dependence between the two partners is so complete that in forest nurseries the appropriate fungus is often introduced into the soil arti-

Mycorrhiza is the fungal equivalent of the nodules that form on the roots of leguminous plants. The picture above shows the roots of the coral root orchid covered with the commonest type of root fungus, endotrophic mycorrhiza, which penetrates into the cells of plant roots. The fungus is important to many plants and especially the heaths, such as those seen on the right, growing in Glen Spean, Scotland.

ficially if it is not already there. The difference between the trees with mycorrhiza and those without can be dramatic. If Virginia pine-tree seedlings grown on Iowa prairie soil are inoculated with mycorrhizal fungi, they can build up twice as much living substance as do similar seedlings with uninfected roots.

One rather interesting fact about the different functions of the two symbiotic associations of root nodules and mycorrhiza has been observed in the forests around Yangambi in Zaïre. The roots of leguminous trees in the very thick Yangambi rain forest are mycorrhizal but have no root nodules; but in the sparser vegetation of an adjacent open forest, the roots are nodulated but not mycorrhizal. The explanation seems to be that in the intense competition for nutrients from the rain-forest floor only mycorrhizas are successful, whereas competition in the open forest is chiefly for nitrogen, which the trees obtain through bacteria-infested root nodules.

Unless you uproot a tree, of course, you cannot tell whether its roots are infected with mycorrhizal fungi. All you can see in any case is a thickening and branching of the young rootlets. In the autumn, however, the telltale sign of some types of mycorrhiza is the appearance near a tree of toadstools.

Certain types of fungi, incidentally, are specific to particular types of tree. For example, the very poisonous fly agaric, with its white-spotted bright red cap, often appears in stands of silver birch, thus betraying the fact that the fungus is in league with the birches' roots. Other genera of fungi that form mycorrhizal associations with trees include the fleshy, often brightly colored *Boletus,* and *Lactarius,* which puts forth a toadstool that yields a white milky substance when its skin is broken.

Although we know less about the kind of mycorrhiza in which the fungus penetrates the roots, it seems clear that heath, heather, bilberry, and other moorland plants need these penetrating fungi for successful growth. Heaths and heathers introduced into a garden where none have grown before may fail if the particular species of fungus they require is not present in the soil. Instead of staying in the root, these

fungi spread throughout the plant, and may even get into the seed of some berries (bilberries, for example), thus ensuring that the fungus will be there when the young plant begins to grow. But this type of mycorrhiza is not always beneficial. Some ecologists, in fact, consider it to be a form of controlled parasitism rather than of symbiosis.

The relationships that we have been examining are, if not always mutually advantageous, at least harmful to neither plant nor microorganism. Now, though, let us consider some examples of associations in which all the profit goes to one party in the arrangement, and the other gets a very bad bargain, often being totally destroyed in the process. The gainer is always the microorganism, the loser always the plant, which becomes diseased as a result of the association. Plant diseases are important in nature and in commerce. In a recent year, the United States Department of Agriculture estimated that diseases of crop plants—most of which could be attributed to fungi and bacteria—caused losses of about $3250 million in America. It has been authoritatively suggested that microbe-induced plant disease costs the world's farmers about 12 per cent of their annual crop.

Although it is chiefly fungi and, to a lesser extent, bacteria that are responsible for this devastation, viruses play an important role.

Many viruses are known by the name of the plant they attack and the kind of disease they cause. Among the well-known plant viruses are the tobacco mosaic, potato X, alfalfa mosaic, tomato bushy stunt, tobacco necrosis, tobacco ring spot, and turnip yellow mosaic. Well over 300 such viruses are known to attack and damage crop plants. Plants infected with a virus commonly grow more slowly than uninfected ones, and the tissues of the stem, roots, flowers, fruits, or leaves usually show distinctive changes. They may change color, and the leaves may become spotty, streaky, or stained with rings of light green, yellow, white, brown, or black; hence the familiar names "mosaic," "mottle," "streak," or "ring-spot" virus.

There is no recovery from virus disease. Although a plant may not be killed outright, it may be so weakened as to be of little use in agriculture and unable to compete with healthy plants in nature. Exactly how viruses infect their hosts and what they do once inside, we shall learn later on when we discuss their associations with animals, for the processes are very similar.

The effects of viral infection are not always altogether bad. In tulips, for example, such infection may cause a variegation in the color of the blooms that enhances their beauty and is therefore much prized. Some varieties of tulip have been maintained for generations in the virus-infected state, with the infection transferred from one generation to the next. But such happy results of viral infection are rare: The more common result in most plants is sickness, possibly followed by death.

Tobacco plants are usually infected with tobacco mosaic virus accidentally by field workers, who carry the infectious particles from plant to plant on their hands. Viruses that attack other crops may be transmitted by animals or through infected soil. The same virus may infect several different kinds of plants, causing different disease symptoms in each, and one virus may have many different strains or subtypes, each producing symptoms of differing severity in plants of the same type.

The bacteria that cause disease in plants are also usually able to attack a wide range of plants and damage each in a different way. Common bacterial diseases include crown gall, which occurs on fruit trees, fire blight, which damages fruit trees (especially pear trees) and ornamental trees, and angular leaf spot, which can kill tobacco plants. All these and many more ailments result from bacterial infection. The fire-blight bacteria are carried from tree to tree by pollinating insects. The bacteria that cause angular leaf spot enter tobacco leaves by means of the stomatal pores, and each bacterial colony then feeds upon, and destroys, a small angular piece of leaf. The bacteria, like the viruses, get their sustenance from the host plant; the disease from which the plant suffers is simply the process of destruction that gives life and energy to the parasitical microorganisms.

The most destructive diseases in plants are caused by fungi, whereas, conversely, the fungi are relatively unimportant in their associations with man and other mammals, from whom it is the viruses and bacteria that exact the highest toll. The associations between plants and fungi that result in disease are either loose relationships, which permit a particular fungus to attack a wide range of hosts, or specific associations, in which a particular fungus owes its existence to its ability to live in or on a single type of host plant and no other.

Fungi attack the roots, leaves, stems, branches, flowers, and ripe fruits of plants. Among the fungi that feed on the roots of plants are those that cause various kinds of potato disease; some that are responsible for a serious disease of pine-tree plantations called butt-rot; and an extremely destructive type that eats into the seedlings of cereal crops. When this latter fungus attacks wheat, it brings on the commercially catastrophic disease known by the appropriate name of "take-all." Fruit trees, too, are extremely susceptible to fungus disease. If you notice that the leaves of your plum trees have a curious silvery look, the tree is infected by *Stereum purpureum,* a fungus that produces purple reproductive structures on the branches that it destroys. Apple trees are affected by a less colorful fungus, which makes its home on the bark and forms a canker that completely encircles the branch.

Some of the fungi responsible for the most severe diseases of crop plants have complex and remarkable life cycles. *Puccinia graminis,* which causes black rust (or stem rust) of wheat, is one such fungus. It produces no less than five different kinds of reproductive spores during its life cycle and depends on a specific and intimate relationship with two totally different kinds of plants for its survival. Let us look at its life cycle in detail.

As black rust, *Puccinia* lives on wheat, but it can get there only via the common barberry. The barberry plant is infected by dispersal spores in the spring; these, the first of the five different kinds of spore, are called *basidiospores.* The airborne basidiospores land on barberry leaves, and germinate in tiny drops of water on the leaf surface by putting out germination tubes, which form a suckerlike structure on the leaf surface. While the edges of the sucker clamp fast to the leaf, the center portion grows until it punctures the surface and gains entrance. Once inside, the fungus produces a branched network of fungal threads, which feed by thrusting fine tubes into the surrounding living cells. Attack by a single basidiospore leads to a local infection only a few millimeters across, and in this spot the leaf cells are not killed; instead, stimulated to new activity, they produce a swollen region. Tiny flask-shaped structures, now appearing on its upper surface, contain a new kind of spore, which is called a *pycniospore.*

The pycniospores are coated with a sugary substance that attracts insects. Then, when an insect carries them from one infected area of the leaf to another, a fertilization process takes place and the fertilized cell develops into a spore-producing structure on the underside of the leaf, which makes still another type of spore: the *aeciospore.* (This exchange of spores is a primitive kind of sexual reproduction, and it is interesting that *Puccinia* should have evolved a mechanism for pollination similar to that developed by flowering plants.) The aeciospores are liberated into the air. They cannot survive on barberry plants even if they land on them. Where they can and do flourish, however, is on wheat.

An aeciospore that lands on a wheat plant germinates in a drop of water on the leaf or stem surface, putting out fine germination tubes that enter the plant through the stomata. The thread-like fungus ramifies through the plant and eventually develops yet another spore-producing structure, which ruptures the outer layer of the wheat leaf or stem in order to disperse its *uredospores.* These are reddish brown and give the diseased plant its characteristic rusted appearance. Uredospores are dispersal spores; like the aeciospores, they can be airborne for long distances without losing their ability to germinate. They can infect only wheat, not barberry. And so the disease is spread from one wheat field to another.

Toward the end of the season, the production of uredospores gives way to the formation of dark-brown *teliospores,* which are resting spores. They remain attached to the wheat stalk and are inactive over the winter. The following spring, they germinate to produce basidiospores again. These thin-walled, short-lived spores can germinate only on barberry leaves, where they start the cycle once more.

Wheat rust is chiefly a problem in the wheat fields of North America. The plant is not killed by the fungus, but its ability to manufacture food is greatly reduced, and it may wilt and shrivel. When harvested, the diseased wheat may throw up great reddish-brown clouds. It is sometimes possible to eliminate the disease by destroying barberry plants in areas around the wheat fields. But even in Canada, where barberry is rare, uredospores may be blown from parts of the United States hundreds of miles away.

Not only can fungus diseases devastate food crops, but they may have unexpected side effects on the people who eat contaminated food. The village of Pont St. Esprit, France, became notorious in 1951 after a number of its inhabitants were struck down by a mysterious illness, characterized in many cases by madness and eventual death. The illness was later diagnosed as ergotism, a poisoning caused by bread made from rye flour infected with ergots, which are the spore-producing structures of a fungus called *Claviceps purpurea*.

It is rarely possible to cure plants that have been stricken with fungal or viral diseases. Prevention, therefore, is the watchword among knowledgeable farmers, who carefully burn dead and diseased branches and plow infected leaves into the ground. Fungicides are useful in controlling a number of such seedborne diseases as loose smut, a disease of oats. But perhaps the most sophisticated technique is use of plants that are inhospitable to the microorganisms.

Some species of barberry, for example, resist colonization by the rust fungus because their leaf surfaces are too thick for the fungal germination tube to penetrate. Furthermore, some plants produce chemical substances that kill the germinating fungus as it lies in its drop of water on the leaf surface. An interesting example of one type of chemical defense is found among the flaxes, some varieties of which can suffer from wilt as the result of a fungal association. The resistant species of flax fight off the invader by producing prussic acid from their roots (albeit in tiny quantities). This not only helps to stop the specific dangerous microorganism from growing in the rhizosphere, but also stimulates another kind of soil fungus to produce certain substances that also destroy the dangerous kind.

Now we have seen something of the ways in which microorganisms live with and on green plants, from the very simple, loose associations that exist in the rhizosphere to the extremely complex life cycle of the rust fungus. We have seen that the organisms of the invisible world can produce highly dramatic effects, often causing their partners to produce specific chemical substances either for defense or for the benefit of both.

In the preceding chapter we considered the influence of free-living microorganisms on the great natural cycles of the earth. Now that we also know how microorganisms are involved in the part played on earth by plant life, our next step is to examine their effect on, and associations with, animals—starting with small animals.

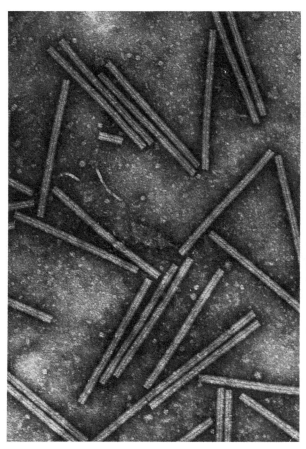

Top: a tobacco leaf infected with the tobacco mosaic virus. The spots are areas of dead cells. Above: electron micrograph of tobacco mosaic virus. Right: the virus is spread accidentally by tobacco plantation workers who carry the invisible infective particles from plant to plant on their hands.

Barberry

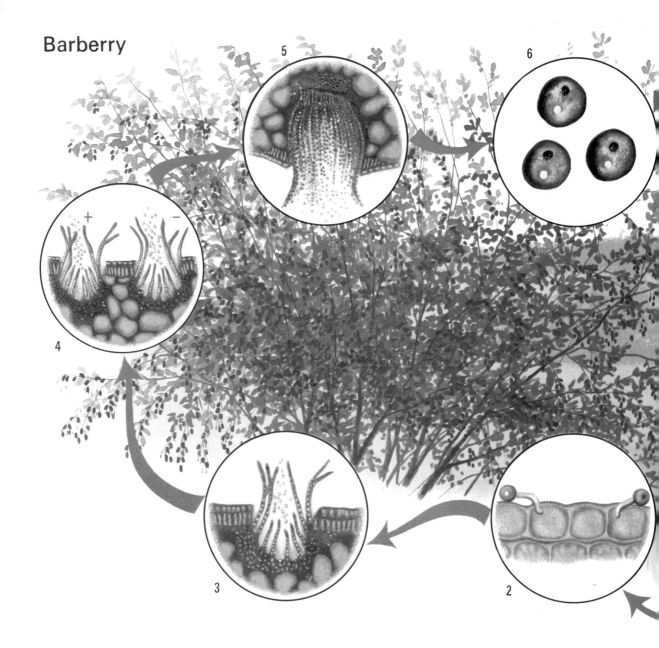

The Life Cycle of Black Rust
(Puccinia graminis)

1 Dispersal spores called *basidiospores* are liberated into the air in spring.
2 Basidiospores germinate on barberry leaves and grow inside leaf cells.
3 Fungal cells multiply to produce structures in which *pycniospores* develop.
4 Pycniospores carried by insects from one infected site to another undergo a process of fertilization.
5 The fertilized cell develops into a structure on the underside of the barberry leaf that produces *aeciospores*

6 The aeciospores are liberated.
7 Aeciospores germinate on wheat stems or leaves and grow through stomata.
8 Structures producing *uredospores* appear on the wheat stem or leaf. These airborne spores infect other wheat plants during the summer.
9 In late summer *teliospores* are produced. These resting spores remain inactive during the winter attached to the wheat stem.
10 The teliospores germinate in the spring to produce basidiospores.

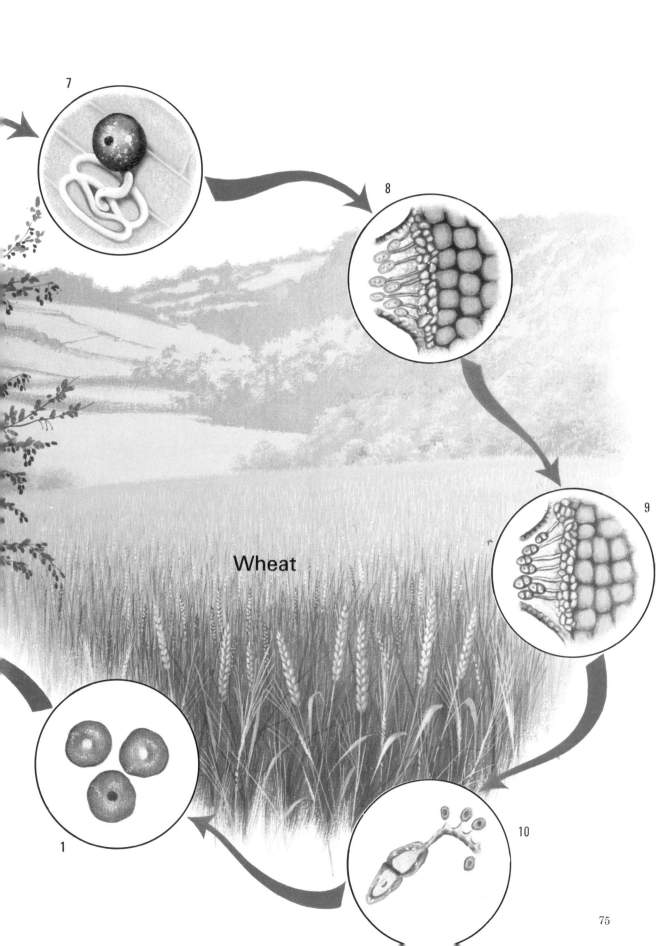

Wheat

Microbes
and Lower Life

> So, naturalists observe, a flea
> Hath smaller fleas that on him prey;
> And these have smaller fleas to bite 'em,
> And so proceed *ad infinitum*.

Jonathan Swift has encapsulated one of the basic truths of biology in these four lines of verse. There is hardly a single living creature that does not play host to some other form of life. The microorganisms live on and with everything that lives, including other microorganisms. Protozoan, alga, fungus, bacterium—each has its microbial partners, welcome or unwelcome.

Only the viruses seem free from colonization. The reason for this is twofold. First, the viruses are totally dependent on other living things for their survival and can carry out their life processes only *inside* other living cells. Secondly, no other creatures are small enough, or would find what the stark viral structure has to offer attractive enough, to make such an association worthwhile.

You might think, by the same argument, that bacteria would also be ruled out as hosts, but in fact they are parasitized by a special kind of virus, the *bacteriophage,* or *phage* for short. In animal bodies, viruses are taken into living cells by a process akin to absorption, but they cannot be similarly absorbed into a bacterial cell, which is invariably surrounded by thick walls that form an effective barrier to marauders. To overcome this defense, the phages have developed a unique method of injecting themselves into bacterial cells, and their bodies have become modified to facilitate the process.

Many phages have both a "head" and a "tail," and the short, thin, tail-like part of the structure has a number of long fibers attached to its lower end. This "tail" is simply a hollow tube, through which the "head" can empty its contents.

One type of bacterium that lives in the human

Aphids, scourge of farmers and gardeners because of their ability to reproduce rapidly, are responsible for transmitting many plant diseases. Without the birds, spiders, ladybugs, and parasites that prey on them, most vegetation would be destroyed.

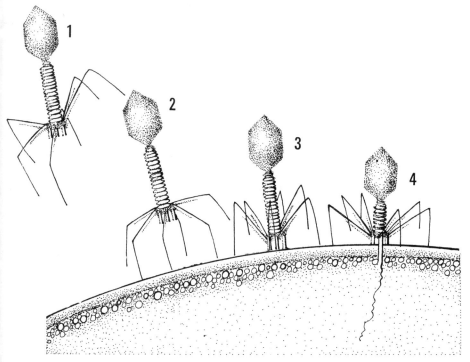

The creature looking like a moon-landing vehicle in the drawings, left, is a bacteriophage, a virus parasitic on bacteria. Stage 1 shows the bacteriophage approaching a bacterium. In stage 2 the tail fibers have made contact with the cell surface. In stage 3, the tail fibers lower the tubular "tail" of the bacteriophage, bringing it into contact with the cell wall. In stage 4, the tail pierces the bacterium's wall and, like a living hypodermic syringe, injects the material from its "head" into the body of the bacterium. The bacteriophage's head contains the hereditary material that will take over the bacterium and direct it to make new phages. Right: electron micrographs of an actual bacteriophage (magnified 650,000 times) illustrate stages 1 and 4 of the diagram at the left.

gut is parasitized by just such a bacteriophage, which has been code-named T4, and of which scientists have made a detailed study. The head of T4 contains the hereditary material—all the information it needs in order to commandeer the living machinery of the bacterium and divert it toward the construction of new phages rather than new bacteria. It was once thought that the phages make their way into the host bacteria by swimming with their tails, approaching the bacterial cell head-first, and chewing their way in. In fact, however, the T4 phage looks rather like a moon-landing vehicle, and recent research has shown that it alights on the surface of its victim like a moon-landing vehicle touching down: tail-first, with the tail fibers attaching themselves to the surface of the bacterium.

Once it has landed, T4 becomes a living hypodermic syringe, and injects its hereditary material into the bacterial cell. The anchored fibers begin to contract, thus bringing the phage's hollow tail into contact with the cell wall. Then in some way that is not understood, but that probably involves the production of a chemical substance, the tail pierces the bacterial wall, and the hereditary material contained in the head is injected directly into the bacterial cell. The empty shell of the virus now falls away and is lost.

There is a big difference between all other kinds of microbial association and the relation-ship of a bacteriophage to a bacterium. The hereditary material of the phage is the only part of it that invades the host cell, unlike other parasitical associations in which whole micro-organisms enter and live in or on their hosts' cells or bodies. There is, after all, no need for the entire organism to enter the host cell, for the life of the phage within the host cell is bound up in what happens between the phage's hereditary material and that of the host.

The phage's hereditary material can behave in either of two ways once it is inside the host cell. If it is a *virulent* phage, it sets to work immediately to direct the machinery of the host cell toward the production of new phages. Exactly how it happens remains obscure, but new phages soon appear in the host cell; and after several hundred have been formed, they are released as the host cell bursts and dies. The bacterium does not burst merely because it becomes overcrowded with phages. Apparently, the phages produce a chemical that breaks down the cell wall from within, just as a chemical in the tail of an infecting phage pierces the wall from outside. Thus the virulent phage invades a bacterium, where it multiplies many hundred-fold, and its progeny kill their host before moving on to infect other bacteria.

The so-called *temperate* phages may behave like virulent phages and destroy the cell they invade, or else their hereditary material may behave

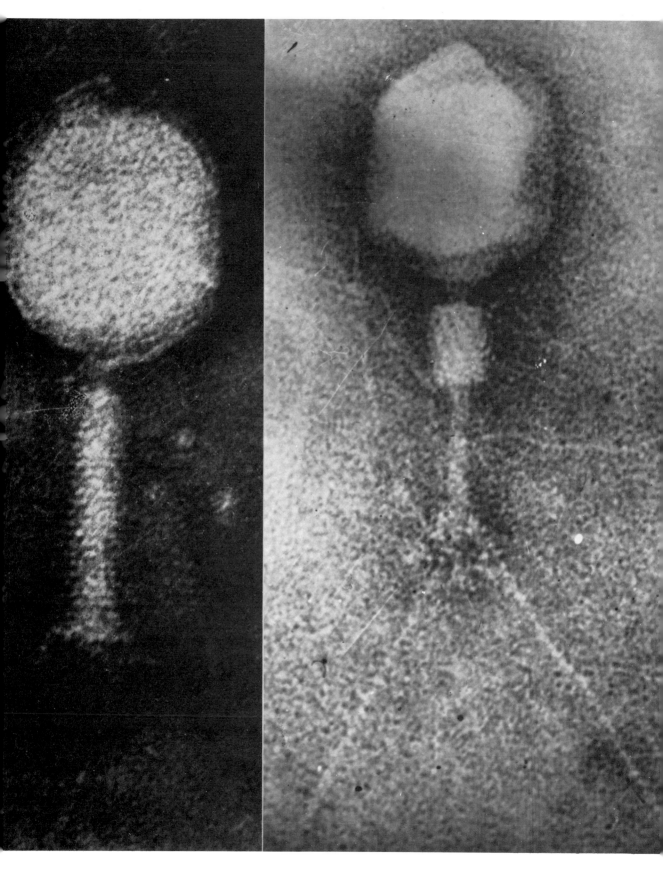

quite differently by becoming combined with the hereditary material of the host. In this latter case, the bacterium continues to live; but when it reproduces itself, it reproduces the phage's hereditary material as well as its own. The particular type of behavior—virulent or temperate—that such phages display depends on the host. Some bacteria evidently permit the combination of their hereditary materials, whereas others do not. If a temperate phage invades a bacterium that is not susceptible to the combined heredities process, the phage destroys the cell while reproducing only itself.

There are certainly few more remarkable associations between organisms than the one in which genetic materials of a phage and its bacterial host are linked together. It is as strange as if a parasitic flea were able to inject its genetic material into a cat, so that the cat's kittens would then have the hereditary characteristics of both animals. And an interesting sidelight is that the temperate phages can add hereditary material not only to bacterial cells, but to animal cells as well. It is thus possible that we may someday learn how to use them to repair genetic defects in higher animals, including man.

For example, one of the numerous diseases caused by faults in the genes of some human beings is galactosemia, a potentially fatal disease that can cause infants to be dwarfed, malnourished, and mentally retarded. It is caused by failure of an individual's cells—or, rather, the hereditary material within the cells—to manufacture a certain chemical necessary for the digestion of certain sugars. Remarkably enough, one bacteriophage, code-named *lambda,* has the ability to produce this very chemical.

In a notable experiment carried out in 1971, when scientists of the National Institutes of Health and Mental Health in Bethesda, Maryland, introduced phage lambda into cells taken from a galactosemia sufferer, the infected cells seemed able thereafter to manufacture the chemical. The phage hereditary material had evidently made good the deficiency in the human hereditary material! It will take many giant steps to proceed from this single, isolated experiment to the wholesale repair of hereditary defects by means of the bacteriophages. But we have at least had a glimpse of a whole new area of exciting medical possibilities.

Let us now turn from the bacteriophage-bacterium association to have a look at some less exotic microbial relationships. The protozoans commonly play host to both bacteria and algae. Some slipper-shaped paramecia appear green from the numerous green algae that they harbor within their single-celled body. These algae, like all green plants, manufacture their own food; in fact, they make much more than enough for their needs. And so, given adequate light, they can keep their protozoan host alive even if it gets virtually nothing else to eat. But if the algae—a species of *Chlorella*—are removed from the paramecium, the protozoan can survive only if it finds additional nutrients. So this is a mutually beneficial association. In return for shelter and transport toward light conditions favorable for photosynthesis, the algae feed their host.

It is a curious fact that the green paramecium eats free-living *Chlorella* algae, yet never harms those inside it. If a paramecium that harbors no algae is brought into contact with some free-living ones of the right species, the algae are taken into the protozoan, and there they multiply—but only until the host has its full complement of permanent guests. The multiplication then stops. Thereafter, if the paramecium meets any free-living *Chlorella* algae, it promptly swallows and digests them. Clearly, the protozoan is able to distinguish between its own algae and others, but nobody yet knows how.

Among the more striking types of association between protozoans and other small creatures, consider the complicated household of *Myxotrichia paradoxa,* a pear-shaped protozoan that lives in close association with four other kinds of living creatures: one insect and three other microorganisms. *Myxotrichia* itself is a guest in the intestine of a certain Australian termite, where it contributes to the insect's survival by helping it digest the pulverized wood on which it lives. A number of long flagella are attached to the narrower end of *Myxotrichia's* cell, and the cell surface is covered by what early observers thought was a mass of shorter flagella. It took a detailed examination to reveal that these shorter hairlike "flagella" are actually long, twisty *spirochetes,* which belong to the bacterial group that includes the microbes responsible for the venereal disease syphilis.

Not only is the surface of the protozoan's cell covered with these creatures, but a large number of smaller bacteria cluster around the spirochetes, and yet a third kind of bacterium lives inside the cell. The spirochetes undoubtedly helps to propel the *Myxotrichia* along, even though it has flagella of its own. Otherwise, it is hard to determine the various benefits that each of these several types of microorganism gets from this web of associations. Quite probably, however, accessibility to food, as well as help in digestion, are among them.

Not many households within the invisible world are as complex as that of *Myxotrichia*. Even superficially simple relationships, though, are sometimes hard to fathom. For example, among the several types of association between different kinds of alga, there is one in which the host cells are green algae that have somehow lost their green pigmentation. Inside these cells, however, are threadlike filaments of a blue-green alga that appears to have taken over the food-manufacturing function of the host's lost green pigments. How does such a relationship develop? The most likely answer is that the host algae probably engulf the blue-green algae as food, but that the "meal" somehow manages to avoid being digested. Instead it apparently remains intact as a permanent source of nourishment.

Sometimes we can only guess at the respective roles of partners in some associations. Yet from time to time we do find new solutions to old mysteries. It never seemed clear what the bacteria contribute to most bacterium-protozoan associations, until scientists discovered that many such associations may be absolutely essential for the protozoan host. We have recently learned that the bacteria that live within at least one flagellate protozoan actually manufacture some of the amino acids that the host cannot make itself. And the amino acids are the basic building-blocks for all proteins.

We have seen that protozoans maintain intimate relationships with green algal cells that provide food for their hosts; with bacterial cells, which perhaps manufacture vital substances; and with spirochetes that are almost indistinguishable from the protozoan's own flagella. All of this lends support to the theory that the living cell of today, whether plant or animal, with all its complex internal structures may have arisen from much simpler ancestral cells that formed increasingly complex associations with other simple organisms.

It now seems probable, for example, that the *mitochondrion,* an ovoid structure found in virtually all cells and responsible for the production of energy, was once a free-living bacterium. Over millions of years, the theory goes, it established an association with the creatures that eventually evolved into today's plant and animal cells—an association that became so intimate that it was maintained and continued even when the cells reproduced.

Many people also believe that flagella and cilia were acquired in a similar way. Such microorganisms as *Myxotrichia* suggest how this might have happened. (In higher animals, some flagella and cilia have been drastically modified to perform utterly new functions. For instance, our own human cells that receive light and detect odors may well have been cilia or flagella in the distant past. And is it not probable that the chloroplasts that contain the pigment chlorophyll in all green plants were derived in some way from early forms of free-living algae?

It is difficult to find conclusive proof for any such theories, and it is indeed unlikely that we shall ever know the full evolutionary story. But the general hypothesis remains highly credible. It seems reasonable to believe that the structures of all the cells that make up the many varieties of plants and animals in the world today are the results of associations among microorganisms hundreds of millions of years ago.

Now let us look at the relationships involving microorganisms and insects. Such relationships are among the most noteworthy of all symbiotic associations. We have already seen how some protozoans live in the intestines of termites. Although termites eat wood, they cannot digest it and are entirely dependent on their microbial partners for this service. The digestive system of the insect is modified to provide a special chamber in which to house the protozoans.

Even more remarkable is the association of certain fungi with the insect world. Some of the relationships are quite simple, others extremely sophisticated. As an example of the simpler sort of relationship—one where the fungus merely lives in the insect's nest—let us take a look at what happens in plant galls. A plant gall is a swelling that sometimes appears on a stem, leaf, or bud, often as a result of insects' having deposited their eggs in the plant. In some way that is not understood, this causes the formation of abnormal plant tissue, which nourishes the insect larvae when they emerge from the eggs. Galls caused by some mosquitolike insects contain fungi, which form a thick layer inside the gall. It is possible that the female insect

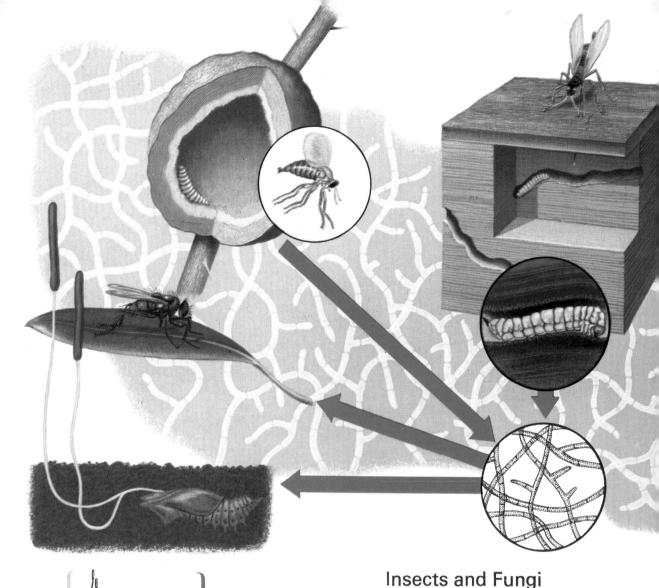

Insects and Fungi

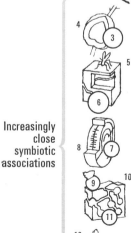

Purely parasitic

Increasingly close symbiotic associations

Fungus not modified by insects

Fungus not always with insects

Fungus modified by insects

Fungus only with insects

1 The fungus *Cordiceps* parasitizing a buried moth pupa.

2 A fly parasitized by the fungus *Entomophora*. A network of hyphae eventually kills the host.

3 An adult gall midge. When the female deposits eggs in a plant a hollow gall develops, and fungal spores laid with the eggs form a layer of fungus on the inside.

4 Gall section showing a midge larva feeding on the fungus layer.

5 A female wood wasp laying eggs by means of a needle-like ovipositor. Fungal spores deposited with the eggs produce hyphae that ramify through the wood.

6 A wood wasp larva. The developing larva burrows into the wood feeding on the fungus as it goes.

7 An ambrosia beetle, feeding on the fungal mycelium, or "ambrosia," that lines its tunnel walls. The fungus develops a yeast-like shape.

8 The pattern of tunnels made by ambrosia beetles in wood. The "cul-de-sacs" house beetle larvae.

9 Ants carrying cut leaves to their nest as compost for fungus gardens.

10 The leaf-cutting ant's nest, showing the fungus gardens.

11 An ant tending a fungus garden. Constant pruning causes the fungus to develop swollen tips.

12 A fungus-growing termite mound with fungus gardens and fruiting bodies.

13 A termite in a fungus garden. Constant "gardening" causes the fungus to produce white balls, which form the termite's food.

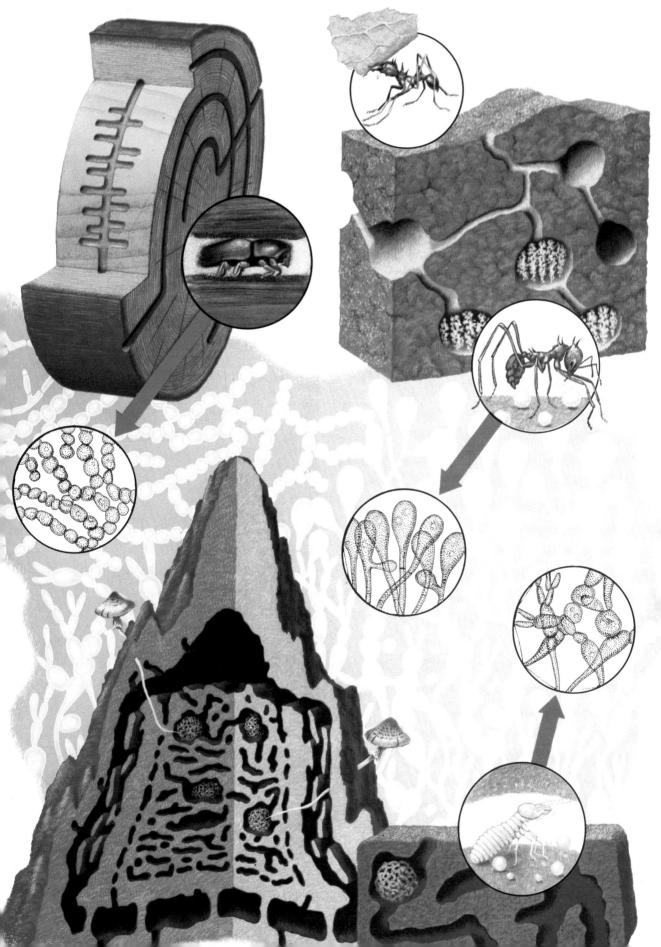

The leaf-cutter ants (left and below) use chewed-up leaf fragments as compost on which to grow their fungus food, whereas the fungus in the opened larval nest or gall (above) is thought to make the gall's woody tissues more digestible for its insect larvae.

Above: termites foraging for food. Termites digest grass, leaves, dead wood, and other materials containing cellulose with the aid of protozoa (below) in their gut. Some species of termite supplement their diet by cultivating fungi in special chambers within their nests (right). These are called fungal gardens.

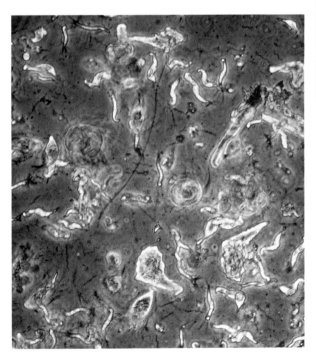

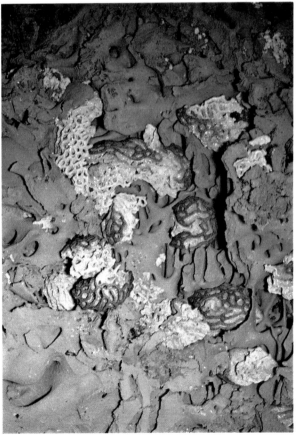

deposits the spores of the fungus at the same time as she lays her eggs. We do not really know what role the fungus plays in the gall. It is unlikely that the larvae feed on it directly; more probably the fungus helps to break down the gall tissue, making it more easily digestible for the young insects.

The gall example illustrates a comparatively loose ecological relationship. A much closer one is enjoyed by another type of fungus and the scale insects that inhabit it. The tiny fungal microorganisms colonize and create a thick lichenlike mat on the leaves and branches of trees, and this habitable mass of fine threads provides shelter from the weather and protection from predatory birds for the scale insects. The insect gets its nourishment from the tree by tapping the sap-carrying veins with a long sucking tube, and the fungus extracts food from insect blood by sending out fine threads to penetrate the bodies of a few of the little animals. The insects invariably suck out more sap than they need, and there is plenty of nourishment for both animal and fungus.

The fungus gets another and equally important benefit from the association. Young scale insects become contaminated with fungal spores while crawling upon the fungal mat; and when they migrate to fresh parts of the tree, they carry the spores with them. These, of course, are the starting points for new fungal growth. Thus the fungus provides shelter for the insects, and the insects provide both food and a means of dispersal for the fungus.

Another animal that rewards its fungal associates for services rendered by helping to disperse it is the wood wasp. The female wasp lays her eggs in damp wood by means of a long, slender ovipositor, at the base of which are tiny pouches containing fungal cells. The cells cling to the deposited eggs and give rise to a mass of fungal threads, which, as they grow into the wood, leave channels filled with fungi. When the larvae hatch, they move along these channels, eating the fungus as they go. The fungus, which feeds on the wood, does not need the wasp for food, only for dispersal; the wasp, however, needs the fungus to help it break down and digest the wood, which it cannot assimilate alone.

Female wood-wasp larvae have small pouches

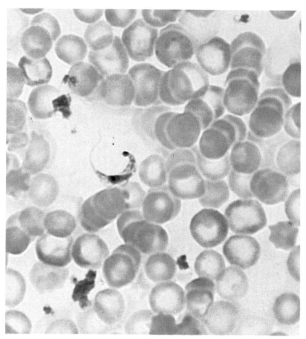

Minute single-celled organisms, such as Trypanosoma *(above), are responsible for a large number of diseases in man. Many of these organisms live part of their life-cycle in insects, part in man and other animals. One of the insect carriers of* Trypanosoma, *which causes anemia and fever in man, is the blood-sucking South American Rhodnius bug (right). The human louse, (left), is the carrier of the organism responsible for typhus*—Rickettsia.

tucked away in a fold between the first and second segments, and small pieces of fungus are trapped by a waxy substance inside the pouches. When the larva becomes a pupa, it loses its pouches, but the adult female picks up flakes of fungus-impregnated wax as she emerges from the pupal skin, and it is these that become lodged in the pouches at the base of the ovipositor. Thus the transfer of the fungus from one generation of wasps to the next is assured.

Some insects actually maintain fungus "gardens"—an outstandingly sophisticated type of microorganism interaction. The ambrosia beetle does this, for example; in small pockets in its hard outer skeleton this wood-boring insect carries some fungal spores. Ambrosia beetles attack hardwood and fallen timber that is moist and filled with sap (Europeans call them "beer beetles" because they sometimes bore into beer and wine kegs). As the beetle bores its way through the wood, fungal spores spill out of the pockets and germinate, so that the tunnel becomes lined with a mass of velvety fungus. The fungal cells feed on the wood of the tunnel, and the fungal mycelium forms the "ambrosia" on which the insect feeds, and for which it is named.

You can distinguish the borings of an ambrosia beetle from those of other beetle species by the black or brown discoloration of the fungal spores that surround the neat, circular tunnel opening. The tunnel contains the beetle's larvae too—either in separate niches or in communal chambers. When the adult insect emerges from the pupa, it feeds on the mass of ambrosial fungus that lines its part of the tunnel; as it eats, it rocks backward and forward, thus making sure that its pockets become filled with fungal spores.

Perhaps the most interesting examples of fungal gardens are the ones tenderly cultivated by certain tropical termites—destructive creatures that do an estimated annual amount of damage to West African buildings equal to 10 per cent of the value of the buildings attacked. These termites invade all manner of materials, from wood to rubber, from growing crops to underground cables. Their nests may be huge mounds of hardened earth or may be completely subterranean. Each such nest contains one or more fungus gardens, which look rather like gray or brownish sponge, often convoluted like

the flesh of a walnut, and which may be very large indeed. A typical garden can measure as much as two feet in diameter and weigh up to 60 pounds. The garden is always enclosed tightly in a cavity lined with a mixture of saliva and dirt; and some species of termites even ventilate their gardens by means of an elaborate system of vertical conduits that extend to the surface of the nest.

The insects tend the gardens diligently. They even fertilize them with manure composed of the partly digested feces of worker termites. And they "weed" the gardens, too, by removing bacteria and alien fungal spores. The termites continually eat away at their gardens, and it seems probable that the fungi help them to digest other materials that they have swallowed; possibly the microorganisms also provide vita-

mins for the insects. The fungus flourishes as a result of its rich diet of termite excrement.

Certain ants, too, are keen fungus gardeners. Among these are the leaf-cutting ants, found only in some of the hotter parts of the Western Hemisphere. One species, which lives in eastern Texas and southern Louisiana, builds nests that may be 50 feet across and 20 feet deep. New nests are initiated by a young queen ant, which carries a small pellet of fungus in a pouch just below her mouthparts. She uses this for starting up a small fungus garden on her excreta, and feeds the fungal matter to the first larvae of the worker ants. When they are mature, the workers forage for such foods as caterpillar excrement, fallen flower parts, and other soft plant debris, and they also cut leaves from trees. Unlike the termite gardeners, these ants do not begin the

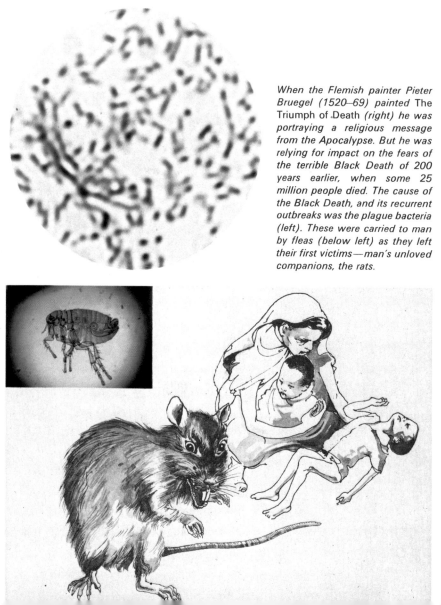

When the Flemish painter Pieter Bruegel (1520–69) painted The Triumph of Death (right) he was portraying a religious message from the Apocalypse. But he was relying for impact on the fears of the terrible Black Death of 200 years earlier, when some 25 million people died. The cause of the Black Death, and its recurrent outbreaks was the plague bacteria (left). These were carried to man by fleas (below left) as they left their first victims — man's unloved companions, the rats.

process of digestion by swallowing the results of their foragings. Instead, they add their findings, chopped into small pieces, directly to the garden—which, in consequence, looks like a gray mass of finely cut bits of plant material held together by threads of fungus.

The adult ants feed on the swollen tips of the threads. These are found in clusters, which, to the naked eye, are barely visible as minute white dots in the garden. (The clusters are known as "kohlrabi" bodies, but they are not to be confused with the vegetable of the same name.) As long as the ants are actively tending their garden, the fungi do not produce fruiting bodies, although they start sending up mushrooms as soon as a nest is abandoned. How the ants impose this sort of birth control on their fungi is not known. Perhaps constant "pruning" inhibits

the development of spore-dispersal structures.

In some insects, bacteria or yeasts actually grow within the body cells, which become specialized for just this function. Such cells are called *mycetocytes,* and although they may be found scattered throughout the body of an insect, they are more often combined together to form special organs. Frequently these organs are merely blind sacs opening into the gut, and the reason for their existence is nutritional. When such insects are deprived of their internal guests, they invariably suffer from lack of vitamins, and sometimes from protein deficiencies as well. Thus, microorganisms are welcome guests in numerous ecological associations because they either help their hosts to digest substances that the hosts cannot tackle, or make substances required for the hosts' well-being.

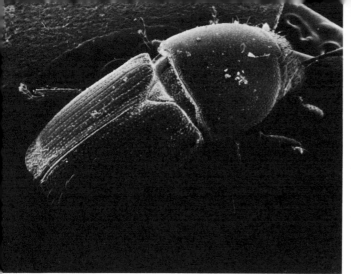

Right: an elm killed by Dutch elm disease. Above: a cross section of an elm-tree stem showing the black spots of fungus that killed the tree and, left, a bark-boring insect that lives on the wood of the elm tree and transmits the fungus.

The microorganisms that live in or on insects often have a significance that goes beyond the biologically interesting nature of the association, because some insects carry disease, and the diseases they carry are usually caused by their invisible partners. The mosquito and many other insects that carry disease-producing microbes to their victims in the course of pursuing their own life activities are said to be *vectors*. There is a wide range of possible associations between a microorganism and its vector. In some cases the relationship is simple and unspecific; in others, the microorganism, the insect vector, and the ultimate victim are essential parts of a complex cycle of infection and disease.

The common housefly is a familiar example of the simple type of relationship. Houseflies are not in themselves harmful, nor do they have any sort of specific association with a harmful microbe. But in their search for food they crawl over decaying matter—often excreta of other animals—which is sure to be a paradise for microorganisms. The microbes stick to the fly's rough skin and to the hairy pads on its feet. Then, when it alights on human food, the microorganisms are transferred to the food, and thence to some hapless victim. Enteric bacteria, which cause diseases of the intestine, are particularly likely to be spread in this way.

We find a much more complex pattern of association when we look for the genesis of rickettsial diseases—those brought on by a bacterium-like organism (which may really be a protozoan) belonging to the genus *Rickettsia*. The rickettsiae cause diseases ranging from Rocky Mountain spotted fever to a mysterious ailment called "Q-fever," but they are best known for causing typhus, a very infectious and often lethal disease.

(Typhus, by the way, is not the same as typhoid, for which a rickettsia is not responsible.) The vector for typhus is a louse—either the human head louse or the body louse. The rickettsias live in the gut of the louse and are liberated in its feces. When the louse bites a person, it may simultaneously defecate onto the punctured skin, thus almost inevitably providing the microorganisms with an entry into the body. If an uninfected louse bites the infected victim, it picks up some rickettsias with its meal of blood, and so can transmit the typhus to another.

Ticks and mites also help to spread rickettsial diseases. Rocky Mountain spotted fever is carried by ticks, which transfer the microorganisms to man. An ailment with the unpleasant name of "rickettsial pox" is carried by mites, which can transfer it to mice or people.

A particularly nasty series of associations is responsible for the dreaded Black Death (or bubonic plague), which destroyed one quarter of Europe's population in the 1300s, and which decimated the population of London in 1665. *Pasteurella pestis,* the bacterium that causes the disease, lives in the bloodstream of rats and is passed along to rat fleas when they suck their host's blood. These fleas attack human beings as well as rats, and so they transmit the plague further in rat-infested places. Bubonic plague remains a menace in some parts of Asia and has been a very serious problem in war-ridden Vietnam during recent years.

Among the other harmful microorganisms passed along by insect vectors, one of the most virulent is the thin, crescent-shaped protozoan that causes sleeping sickness. It is transmitted to man by the tsetse fly, a bloodsucking fly found only in Africa. The protozoan lives initially in

Left: peach-tree leaves affected with leaf-curl fungus. There are many fungi that attack plants and cause great damage to commercial crops. Plant diseases can be spread in many ways including grafting healthy parts on to diseased plants, and propagating from the seed of diseased plants. The most common cause, however, is by transmission through insects, such as the noctuid moth (right) which, when puncturing the protective skin of the peach to obtain the nutritious juices, allows fungus spores to enter the fruit.

the gut of the fly, but it soon invades the salivary glands and the mouthparts, from where it is injected into a human host when the fly takes a meal. In man it lives and grows chiefly in the bloodstream, but in the latter stages of the disease it invades the brain and spinal cord.

The viruses are less likely than protozoans to be passed along to man by infected insects, although there *are* a few viral diseases that human beings can catch in this way. Fleas, however, do carry one of the best-known viral diseases of animals, myxomatosis, which killed most of western Europe's rabbits a few years ago. There are very specific associations here between both the virus and its host flea and the flea and its host. When an infected rabbit dies in its crowded burrow, the fleas quickly leave the dead body, in search of other hosts. When they find a new host they expel their viral parasites into the victim's body through their mouthparts. Curiously enough, though, there is a less virulent form of this virus that is carried by a mosquito. A rabbit bitten by an infected mosquito is in the same category as a person inoculated with cowpox: it becomes immune to the more dangerous disease because the less harmful disease calls forth the right antibodies.

Insect vectors carry destructive microorganisms to plants as well as to animals. Dutch elm disease, a modern scourge that threatens the entire elm population of both the Old and the New World, is caused by a fungus that effectively starves trees by blocking up the channels through which the plant's food and water must flow. This fungus is transmitted by bark-boring beetles, which live on elm wood and carry fungal spores about with them in much the same fashion as do the ambrosia beetles. By cultivating fungal gardens in their brood tunnels, the bark beetles bring death to the elms, which have no built-in defenses against their killers.

Insects are particularly important as vectors in the spread of viral diseases of plants. Such diseases often result from a very simple form of association in which an insect with biting mouthparts feeds on an infected plant and carries away the virus smeared on its proboscis. Thus it becomes a kind of "unwitting" vector. Such casual associations are typical of a number of different species of aphid. The aphids are probably responsible for transmitting the great majority of plant viral diseases; one species alone is the vector of 50 different viruses. Of several major types of aphid-virus association, the simplest consists of the mechanical transmission of the virus from one plant to another on the mouthparts of the aphid. No biological association is involved, and usually only the first

plant attacked is actually infected by the virus.

More complex is the "circulative" type of behavior. Here the aphid again merely picks up a virus from a diseased plant, but another plant cannot be infected until the virus has passed through the insect's gut, into its bloodstream, and back to the salivary glands.

A third and much more complex pattern involves the so-called "propagative" virus, which has a definite biological association with its host and lives and multiplies within the aphid's body. An example is the virus that causes leaf roll in a number of plants. An aphid infected with leaf-roll virus is able to pass it on to a susceptible plant even after seven days of feeding on a plant such as cabbage, which is immune to leaf roll, whereas other types of virus would have been destroyed in the insect's body in that time.

In some plant diseases there is cooperation among three creatures—an aphid and two viruses. One such three-way association is responsible for "rosette disease," which results in the discoloration and deformation of tobacco plants. In this ailment, one microorganism (the mottle virus) depends on the presence of another (the vein-distorting virus) to enable it to be picked up and transmitted by an aphid. Precisely what this sort of cooperation involves is as yet a mystery to microbiologists.

Plant virus diseases are spread not only by bark beetles and aphids, but also by many other creatures, such as mites, eelworms, and even fungi, but we do not always know *how*.

The vectors themselves do not always get off scot-free, of course, for they are frequently struck down by their invisible associates. For example, there is one bacterium that produces a poisonous protein that crystallizes around its spores, with lethal results for the larvae of butterflies and moths. Larvae that swallow these bacteria are quickly paralyzed, for the poison drastically affects the ability of the larva's intestine to absorb food and water. The bacterial spores then germinate and feed on their unfortunate hosts, which soon die.

So effective is this poison against over 100 species of moth that it is now being used as an insecticide. The bacteria are grown in large fermentation vessels, and a concentrate consisting of spores and poisonous crystals is prepared and used as a dust or spray on larvae-infested plants. This concentrate seems to be harmless to human beings and livestock. Some authorities believe that there may be great possibilities in the use of other such poison-making bacteria as a new approach to insect control.

About 200 viral diseases of insects have been identified, all of them affecting chiefly the

There are many examples of the beneficial associations between marine creatures and microorganisms. One of the most startling is the association between certain fish and luminous bacteria. The angler fish (above), for instance, uses luminous bacteria to lure its prey into its jaws. Right: the blue coloration in this close-up of the mantle of the giant Tridacnid clam, found on Australia's Great Barrier Reef, is made up of colonies of algae living in the clam's tissues. Light is concentrated on to the chlorophyll-rich algae by the many tiny lenses in the mantle. As the algae multiply they are absorbed as a food supplement by the clam. Far right: photomicrograph showing green alga that has lost its chlorophyll-producing cells. Filaments of the blue-green algae can be seen apparently substituting for the host's missing cells.

larval stages. The larvae may become infected by feeding on plants contaminated by other larvae that have been killed by viruses. There are also many protozoan-engendered and fungal ailments of adult insects.

Before we move on to examine in the next chapter the many kinds of association that exist among microorganisms and mammals, let us glance briefly at just two or three of the interesting living relationships with some creatures not yet mentioned—specifically, with one bird and with a few marine organisms.

Certain birds that are native to Africa and India are called honey-guide birds because they guide ratels, or honey badgers, and other animals—or people, for that matter—to bees' nests. The bird's aim is to have the nest ransacked—not, strangely enough, so that it can have a share of the honey, but so that, after the larger animal has helped itself to the honey, the

bird can eat the broken remains of the wax honeycomb. Even more strangely, the honey-guide bird cannot digest the wax it craves; it must rely on the presence in its alimentary tract of two kinds of microorganism, one a bacterium, the other a yeast. Working in partnership, these microorganisms are able to break down the wax and render the products available to the bird. The delicacy of the association can be judged from the fact that the bacterium could not do its part of the breaking-down job effectively without the help of a certain chemical substance produced by the bird and present in its alimentary canal.

And so from land to water, with a quick look at some examples of aquatic associations. More than 100 different kinds of invertebrate, including jellyfish, corals, sea anemones, flatworms, sponges, and clams, are known to have symbiotic relationships with algae. One very

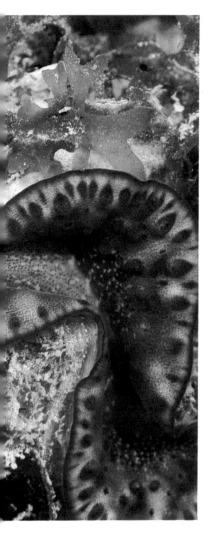

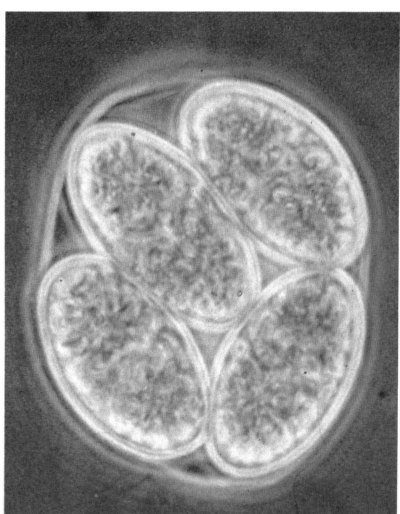

specialized association, found on the Great Barrier Reef of Australia, is the relationship between a type of large clam, the tridacnid clam, and certain yellow or greenish brown algae.

Tridacnid clams have much thicker layers of tissues lining the two halves of their shells than clams usually do, and the algae are concentrated in these tissues. Groups of cells that contain the algae are arranged into conical protuberances that are associated with transparent cells. These transparent cells act as lenses, whose purpose is to focus daylight onto the chlorophyll-rich algal cells so as to enable them to make food. As the algal population in the clam grows, the clam roots out and digests the excess cells.

Some aquatic animals harbor microorganisms for quite unusual purposes. Cuttlefish, some squids, and a number of fishes have special organs that house luminous bacteria. For deep-sea fishes, the light emitted by the bacteria is no doubt an assistance to navigation in the dark water; other species use the light as a signal for mutual recognition. One species of squid is even able to control the intensity of the light, because the organ that houses the bacteria is embedded in the squid's ink sac and partly enclosed by reflective tissues. By changing the position of the dense ink sac in relation to the reflective tissue, the squid can darken or brighten the light. In the luminous fishes, bacteria-housing organs are found under the eyes, on the lower jaw, on the belly, or around the rectum.

In this chapter we have seen microorganisms at work as biochemical warriors (bacteriophages attacking bacteria), digestive aids (gut bacteria of insects), and living headlights (luminescent bacteria in fish) among a host of such other roles as carriers of disease. All these examples are evidence of the amazing variety of parts the microbes play to ensure their survival.

Microbes
and Mammals

Healthy children at play are a commonplace sight in our present-day Western world. Under a century ago, the lethargy of the gravely ill child was just as familiar. The transformation largely reflects mounting medical knowledge of and mastery over the microbes that flourish unseen both on and in our bodies.

Human beings are self-centered creatures. Our own lives, the things we do to fill them, and our health are what matters most to us, and any threat to our well-being provides the best possible impetus for us to search for the source of the trouble and try to root it out. Disease is just such a threat. Ever since it became clear in the middle of the 19th century that microorganisms are responsible for most diseases, scientists have mounted an extensive campaign to discover why various organisms cause various diseases and how to combat them. Of all associations

between microorganisms and animals, therefore, we know most about those that involve man.

It is natural to think of microorganisms chiefly as an agent of disease—as "germs"—but this is only a small part of the complete story. Healthy animals (including man) play host to a wide range of microorganisms, some potentially dangerous and some not, without developing symptoms of disease. In fact, it is often very hard to determine whether the relationship between a microorganism and a higher animal is harmful, beneficial, or neutral. It all depends on the circumstances. In your nose and throat, for example, there are almost certainly microorganisms that can cause diphtheria or pneumonia. That they do not do so except in unusual circumstances (when the body's defenses are weakened, for instance) is a tribute to the remarkable system of checks and balances that enables man and microbe to live in close harmony.

In healthy individuals, microorganisms are chiefly found living on exposed parts of the body. The skin is quite obviously one such region—although, as we shall see, the actual surface of

the skin is less hospitable to microlife than are its pores and crevices. Another, less obvious habitat is the linings of the digestive system, which, like those of the tubes leading from the nose to the lungs, are also exposed, because the digestive system is merely a tube running through the body from mouth to anus. Thus, the contents of the tube remain effectively outside the body unless they are absorbed through the wall of the tube.

For many varieties of microorganism, the digestive system is the most suitable of all places to live, providing, as it does, a steady supply of food for its microscopic residents. Furthermore, the temperature and amount of moisture present in the digestive system of a healthy animal are ideal for microbial growth. Small

wonder, then, that no other single habitat contains such a concentration of microorganisms of so many different kinds. "Single habitat" is perhaps a misleading term, because a mammal's digestive system encompasses a huge variety of different habitats, each harboring its own specialized kind of microbe. In studying the ecology of plants and higher animals, the separation between biologically different habitats is likely to be measured in yards or miles. But the distance between two different habitats that support entirely distinct kinds of microorganism may be only a few thousandths of an inch.

Despite the apparently easy living that the digestive system seems to offer, it is not suited to all species of microbe, for mammals have a

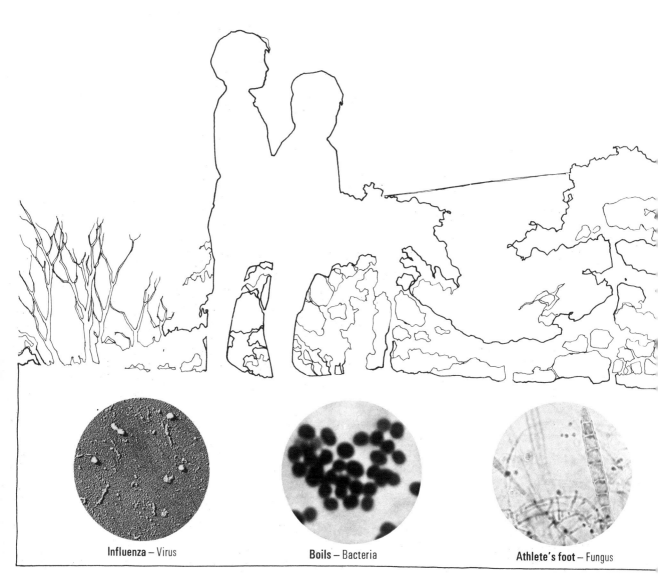

Influenza – Virus   Boils – Bacteria   Athlete's foot – Fungus

range of defense mechanisms that work together to prevent the invasion of harmful micro-organisms as well as to control the number of those allowed to take up residence. Among the defenses is the presence of special cells that can swallow up and destroy microbial trespassers, and the body also produces chemical substances especially designed to kill off intrusive forms of life. We shall examine these defenses more carefully when we take a closer look at disease-causing microbes.

Only such organisms as can overcome or come to terms with the body's defensive mechanisms are able successfully to colonize man and other mammals. But do not assume that all the micro-organisms that live in or on higher animals must continually fight to sustain their position.

The microbiologist's microscope puts human life in a new and unfamiliar perspective. Through this instrument we learn that flesh and blood play host to a miniature world of wildlife— some of it hostile, some neutral, some even beneficial to us. Below are photomicrographs of a few kinds of "enemy" germ that can thrive on or in the body and create disease if they multiply sufficiently. Most bring mere discomfort, but at least one kind is often fatal. Fungi producing ringworm and athlete's foot attack the skin: common ringworm shows as red, round, often itchy patches on non-hairy skin; athlete's foot is an inflammation and cracking between toes. Staphylococcus bacteria entering a sweat gland may form a boil—a painful raised round abscess. Tetanus bacteria penetrating the skin through an open cut give off poisons and trigger severe muscle spasms that can kill if left untreated. Yet other disease organisms are breathed in with droplets in the air. These germs spread down through the body's respiration system, then get into the bloodstream, causing general malaise. Two such kinds of germ are the viruses responsible for influenza and measles. Headache, shivering, and aching are common influenza symptoms. Measles produces a spotty rash, sniffles, a high temperature, and exhaustion.

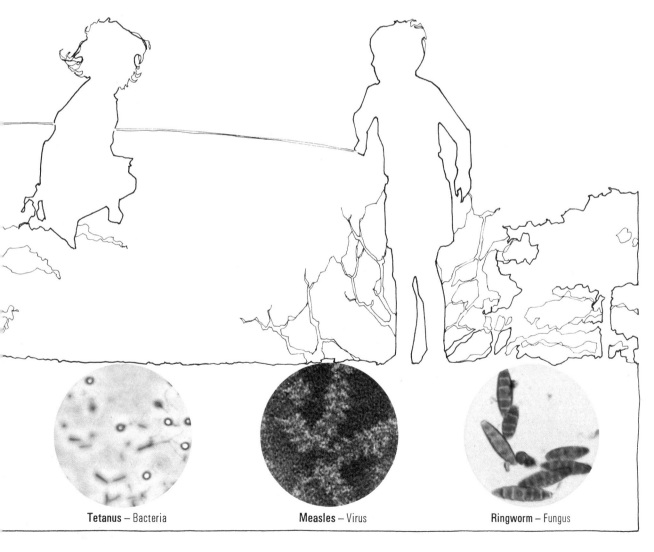

Tetanus – Bacteria   **Measles** – Virus   **Ringworm** – Fungus

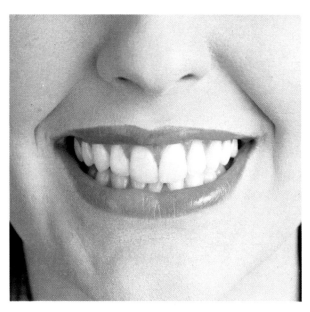

Gleaming, intact sets of teeth like this have become scarce in "developed" nations where sugary foods encourage bacteria whose acid wastes cause tooth decay. Right (greatly enlarged): the branching, knobbly surface of plaque—a bacterial mass found on teeth. Plaque can be kept at bay by frequently brushing the teeth and probing between them with a toothpick.

Some are so beneficial to the host that it has developed ways of encouraging a peaceful and mutually profitable coexistence.

Each region of the digestive system has a distinctive array of microbial inhabitants. First, there is the mouth. Here the immediate threat to the survival of microbial colonizers is the saliva, which, apart from being poor in the kinds of substances on which microorganisms can feed, contains chemicals that can kill them. The teeth appear to be the most important factor in determining what kinds of bacterium are found in an animal's mouth, for teeth provide firm surfaces on which food particles collect and microbes can grow; and the teeth are not in themselves able to attack microorganisms either chemically or physically. Bacteria on the teeth form a tenacious coating—the so-called dental *plaque*—which resists even hard brushing. Plaque is constructed of fine, threadlike bacteria woven together into a dense mat, which in unbrushed places can be as much as 60 times the thickness of an individual bacterial cell.

Bacteria are not the only microorganisms that live in the mouth; it is commonly inhabited by protozoans and fungi as well, including an amoebalike protozoan that lives in and around the gums and feeds on the bacteria it finds there. But bacteria are the chief factor in tooth decay. They gather in the cracks and crevices spared by the toothbrush and the self-cleaning action of tongue and lips, and there they feed on particles of food. They break these down chemically, deriving energy for themselves, but the products of the process, a variety of acidic substances, attack the enamel tooth surfaces.

Once the hard enamel has been breached, further chemical substances produced by bacteria insidiously destroy the inner matter of the teeth. Enamel that contains the chemical fluoride as part of its structure is particularly resistant to the acids formed by bacteria, and this is why many dentists maintain that fluoride should be added to drinking water. The teeth of

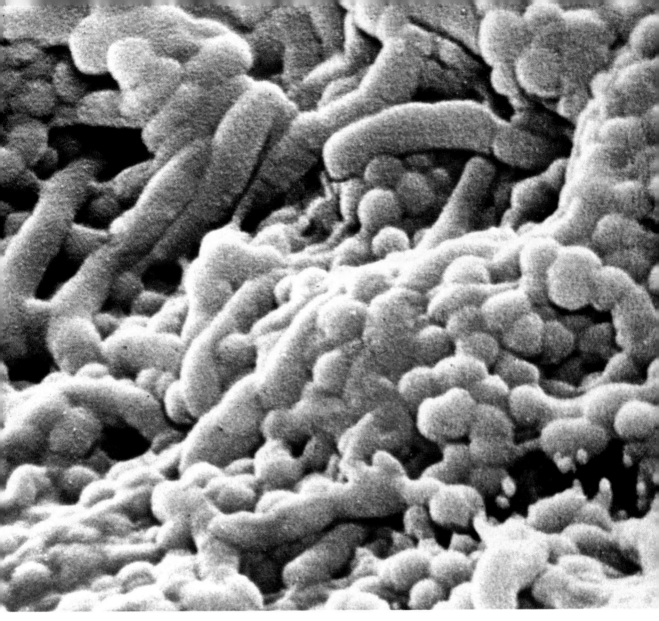

some animals are more resistant to tooth decay than are those of human beings; dogs, for example, have few dental problems because their teeth are shaped in such a way that food particles cannot lodge in the crevices.

It is an interesting fact that the threadlike bacteria of dental plaque are not found in the mouths of human babies during the toothless early months, but take up residence as soon as the teeth begin to appear. Babies in the womb are completely free from bacteria; yet within hours of birth they have the beginnings of a characteristic bacterial population. The baby gets its microorganisms first from its mother during the passage down the birth canal and later by contact with the world outside. The bacterial populations in the gut of the newborn

child are, however, rather different from those that develop later on—a reflection of changing diets. The digestive system of breast-fed infants contains only one type of bacterium, whereas bottle-fed infants are hosts to quite a large range of microorganisms. As the child grows older and its diet changes, the kinds of microorganisms that its digestive system will support also increase and change. But we still know very little about how even the commonest of microorganisms have adapted to survive in the digestive tract.

Partly digested and macerated food passes from the mouth to the stomach, which contains acids strong enough to blister a human hand—and certainly strong enough to discourage the growth of most bacteria. The stomach is therefore

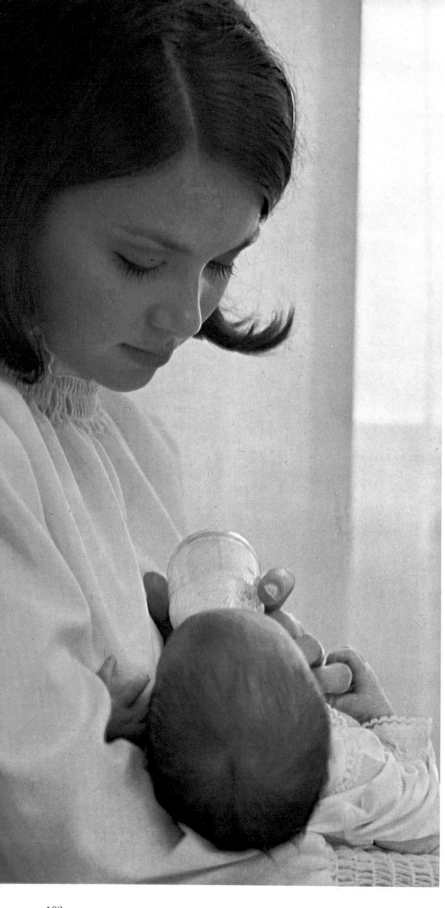

The quantities and kinds of micro-organism that live in a man's digestive system change from human infancy to adulthood. Newborn babies are largely germ free, and acid in the digestive systems of breast-fed babies helps to kill off microbes. But a bottle-fed baby (left) soon acquires a variety of intestinal bacteria—many sucked in from the baby's food container. By adulthood, the human gut has a flora of usually harmless and beneficial bacteria. Densest concentrations flourish in the large intestine (part of which appears in section in the photomicrograph above). There, the bacteria yield gases and other wastes by breaking down food substances that had escaped absorption by the small intestine. More importantly for man, certain bacteria in the large intestine produce nutritionally valuable quantities of riboflavin and other vitamins.

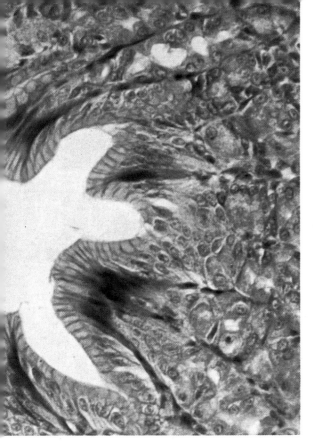

an effective barrier, normally preventing dangerous bacteria from gaining access to the intestines. Nevertheless, large numbers of acid-resistant bacteria and a few fungi are able to make their home in the stomach. And when its normal condition is disturbed—in cases of stomach cancer, for example—it may become less acidic, and thus may allow the free growth of yeasts and bacteria.

Where the small intestine leaves the stomach, it too is very acidic, and so the kinds of microorganisms found there are much like those of the stomach. But the acidity declines and the number of microorganisms increases toward the lower end of the small intestine, just before the beginning of the large intestine. If the stomach is a barrier to microorganisms, the large intestine is a paradise; they are there in enormous numbers. Some live within the mass of digesting food that passes through the intestine, and these microorganisms are eventually expelled along with the fecal material, every ounce of which can contain as many as 300,000 million of the tiny creatures.

But if the bacterial population of the large intestine is to remain fairly constant, the millions of bacteria voided with the feces must be replaced. Here the microbes' salvation is their speed of reproduction. Food takes about 24 hours to pass through the digestive system; in that time the bacteria in the digesting mass may double or quadruple their numbers.

One type of bacterium, which inhabits the inner wall of the intestine, has a distinctive, elongated, threadlike shape, which you would easily recognize if you examined a portion of the large intestine under a microscope. These bacteria do not need oxygen to live (and this is just as well, for there is none in the large intestine). There are also likely to be a few species of protozoan in the digestive tract of a healthy human being. One such protozoan, *Entamoeba histolytica,* appears to thrive in the intestines of a high percentage of people who live in places where sanitation is poor. In most cases it seems to do no harm. In a few individuals, however, it damages the intestines and leads to an unpleasant disease called *amoebic dysentery*.

For a dramatic example of how such an association can benefit the host instead of doing damage, consider the digestive systems of such grass-eaters (herbivores) as the horse, pig, porcupine, rabbit, and guinea pig. These mammals, which depend on green plants for their nourishment, cannot digest cellulose, the tough material that forms plant cell walls. They have overcome this problem by developing a special region of the intestine for the sole purpose of housing colonies of microorganisms that can break the cellulose into simpler substances that the host animal can use. This special organ—the *caecum*—is a saclike, blind extension of the large intestine, inhabited by bacteria and protozoans.

Foodstuffs pass down the intestine and into the caecum. Here the cellulose is broken down by the microorganisms, and the energy contained in the food thus becomes available to both the microbe and its host. One drawback for the host is that because the caecum is a blind alley situated toward the hind end of the gut, much of the foodstuff does not have a chance to be fully broken down by the bacteria; and so a good deal of valuable nourishment is excreted

Some herbivores, such as rabbits and guinea pigs, partly overcome this problem by eating their excrement—an interesting practice known as *coprophagy*. The fecal matter that has passed through their bodies only once is soft and moist. Wild rabbits void this during the day when they are below ground, then immediately eat it again and digest what nourishment remains.

During the second passage, most of the water is extracted. This is why the rabbit pellets that you see around grassy places where rabbits are common are hard and dry.

The most efficient and highly developed system for using microorganisms to supplement mammalian digestive processes—digestion by proxy, as it were—is to be found among *ruminants*: cattle, sheep, goats, and their relatives. These animals get their collective name from the *rumen,* which is a special organ that houses gut microorganisms. Because of the economic importance of cattle and sheep, rumen microbiology and biochemistry have been extensively studied, and we know a lot about the system.

To begin with, the rumen is an extension of the esophagus (the tube that connects the mouth to the stomach), which makes it a sort of first stomach—the first part of the digestive system to receive food after it has been swallowed. The rumen is very large, with a capacity of over 20 gallons in cows and over one gallon in sheep, and it has a complex structure. When food enters the rumen, it becomes mingled with the resident microbial population, consisting chiefly of bacteria and protozoans. The role of the protozoans—which seem to be mostly ciliates—is not fully understood. They apparently play some small part in digesting the food, but their chief function may well be related to the control of the bacteria in the rumen by gobbling up the surplus.

The rumen bacteria are fermenters; indeed, the rumen itself is a large fermentation chamber in which the bacteria convert cellulose into sugars, and then convert the sugars into a number of organic acids. These acids are absorbed through the wall of the rumen into the bloodstream and thus become the chief source of energy for the ruminant. This is a very different form of digestion from that of most mammals, whose digestive systems produce chemicals that convert carbohydrates in their diet into sugars for direct absorption into the bloodstream through the wall of the gut.

As the microorganisms break down the sugars into their component acids, they produce, as a by-product, large quantities of carbon dioxide and methane gas—as much as 45 gallons a day, in fact. And all this gas must be expelled by belching (a process sometimes delicately termed *eructation).* Belching in ruminant animals is more than a mere occasional hiccup. The walls of the rumen undergo two quite separate kinds

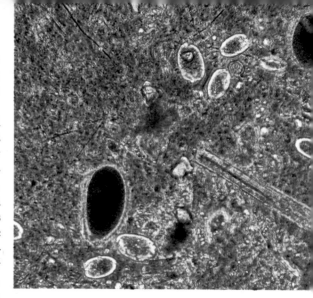

Countless tiny microbes like the protozoans in the photomicrograph above helped this cow to build up its large body. Inside its digestive system, bacteria (their numbers controlled partly by protozoan predators and partly by digestive juices) transform grass to simple energy-producing substances. The bacteria then serve as a body-building protein.

of contraction. One of these serves to mix the contents of the rumen together; the other, a forward-moving contraction, causes the animal to belch. If the gases are not released from the digestive system (as sometimes happens), the animal becomes bloated and dies.

Efficient as the rumen bacteria are at converting cellulose into nourishing acids, they cannot entirely finish the job. Coarse food materials that the microbes have not broken down are returned to the animal's mouth to be chewed again—which is the process of rumination ("chewing the cud"). What happens is that food particles not fully fermented by the bacteria scratch against the sensitive walls of the rumen, causing its upper end to open and permit a ball of undigested food to be sucked into the esophagus and up to the mouth. The food is once again chewed, swallowed, and worked upon by the microorganisms. After a short period, the entire process is repeated.

To keep healthy, mammals need not only carbohydrates for energy but also proteins, fats, and vitamins for growth. So far in our story the ruminant has been supplied only with the necessary carbohydrates by its bacterial partners. They, of course, have been using some of the energy they gain from the fermentation of cellulose to grow and reproduce, and their growth inevitably involves the manufacture of

proteins, fats, and vitamins. After fermentation in the rumen, the food is passed on to what in other mammals would be described as the true stomach. And just as in other mammals, the stomach acids kill most of the residual bacteria in the food mass. The mixture of partly digested food and dead bacteria passes into the intestines, and the animal absorbs what it needs from the mass. So, in fact, it is the *bacteria* that the ruminant digests which provide it with the essential vitamins, fats, and proteins.

In a sense, therefore, many herbivorous animals maintain their own herds of micro-organisms, allowing them to graze and fatten in an especially constructed pasture, and killing them off and digesting them after they have done their work. No similar system for breaking down cellulose exists in man, and we do not digest that part of whatever green vegetables we eat. Cellulose in our diet is chiefly of value as "roughage"—bulky material that helps to keep the muscles of the digestive system in trim.

Microorganisms are found in large numbers in the human nose and throat, in the passages leading to the urinary and reproductive organs, and on the skin. The outer surface of the skin is not a very comfortable place for the microbes, because it is exposed to the atmosphere, which dries it up, and most microbes thrive best in fairly moist habitats. Only the scalp, the areas of the face that bear hair, the passages leading from the ears to the ear drums, the underarm, urinary, and anal regions, and the spaces between the toes are sufficiently moist to support appreciable microbial populations. On this simple fact rests the multimillion-dollar deodorant industry.

There would be no need for deodorants if it were not for the association of skin micro-organisms with a particular type of human sweat gland: the apocrine. Apocrine glands, found chiefly under the arms and around the genitals, are inactive in childhood and begin to operate only when puberty is reached, which explains why adults have a body-odor problem and children do not. There are other sweat glands that produce perspiration for cooling the body, but these seem comparatively free from microorganisms, perhaps because of a continual flow of fluid, which keeps the pores clear. Around the apocrine glands, however, bacteria grow in large numbers. They live on substances in the sweat, and it is their digestive activity that causes the odor. Sweat collected from apocrine glands that are free of bacteria has been found to be odorless, but it begins to smell when bacteria from the skin are introduced into it. Deodorants are really disinfectants that kill the bacteria that live on stale sweat.

Although appreciable populations of micro-organisms can thrive only in moist areas of the skin, some of the invisible creatures do inhabit the entire skin surface, especially in and around the hair follicles (the fine sheaths in which hair shafts are embedded). These channels in the skin provide a first-rate environment for microbial growth. Each hair follicle has a small gland that produces an oily lubricant for the hair shaft. Yeast and other fungi, as well as bacteria, find this an attractive habitat; and large numbers of microorganisms embed themselves around the follicle, just under the skin surface, where they stay firmly attached and cannot be removed by washing. Doctors and others who have to keep their hands and arms scrupulously sterile use a variety of chemicals to remove bacteria.

How densely populated is the human skin? Scientists at the University of Pennsylvania report that in adult males the underarm bears the greatest concentration, with an average population of 15.54 million bacteria per square inch of skin. The scalp and the forehead have estimated average counts of 9.42 million and 1.29 million bacteria per square inch respectively. (Note the huge difference between the numbers on the moist, protected, hair-covered scalp and the more exposed forehead.) By contrast, comparatively few microorganisms appear to live on the back, which houses an estimated average of only 2025 per square inch.

The skin, like the stomach, produces acidic substances that kill off some of the most harmful types of bacterium. Among the few resistant groups are the staphylococci, which are generally present in colonies resembling miniature bunches of grapes. One such bacterium, which lives on the skin of about 10 per cent of all healthy people, can damage sweat glands and hair roots, particularly in adolescence. It is at least partly responsible for acne—the unsightly spots and pimples that blight so many teenagers' hopes of physical beauty (and that have therefore opened up another profitable market for the cosmetic and pharmaceutical industries).

Although vast numbers of bacteria also live in the nose, throat, and nasal passages, very few are able to make their way down to the lungs. The

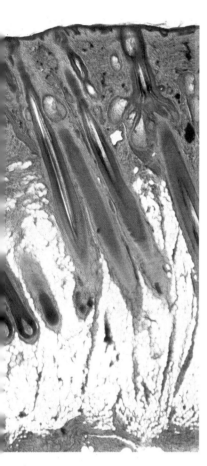

Certain areas of the skin provide favorite homes for microorganisms. Bacteria and fungi are especially numerous just below the surface in the kinds of site revealed by the skin section above. There, microbes find safe niches in the protected shafts (oil-lubricated by associated glands) from which hairs grow. Many microorganisms on skin escape casual detection. But the stale sweat from underarm apocrine glands provides food for bacteria that produce unpleasant body odor. Deodorants applied as spray (right), cream, powder, or a solid stick prevent body odor by killing the bacteria or by inhibiting perspiration (in which case they are known as antiperspirants). Aluminum chloride, petrolatum, formaldehyde, and vinegar are among the chief weapons used in the modern arsenal of anti-odor toiletries.

reason for this can be found in the physical structure of the walls of the air passages that lead from the nose to the lungs. These have a coating of sticky mucus, in which most of the microbes that we take in with every breath are trapped. Moreover, the walls are lined with whiplike cilia, and these beat rhythmically in an upward direction, pushing the inhaled organisms back toward the nose and throat, where they are expelled in the saliva and nasal mucus. A few kinds of organism, however, are so small and light that they escape this sticky fate. The bacterium that causes tuberculosis is one such invader. In most individuals any such bacteria that manage to reach the lungs are immediately engulfed and destroyed by special defensive cells, the *phagocytes*. But in people with low resistance the bacteria can survive and cause tuberculosis.

One unsolved puzzle still blocks our understanding of the relationship between microorganisms and higher animals: why are microbes that seem harmless to one individual deadly to another? Why is it that some individuals can tolerate the presence of large numbers of dangerous microorganisms without succumbing to disease, whereas others capitulate at once.

So far, we have looked chiefly at microorganism–higher animal interactions in which little damage is commonly caused as a result of infection, or in which there may indeed be advantages to both parties. Now let us center our attention on the microorganisms that behave in the way that most concerns us as human beings—the ones that impose disease and death upon us. Of the five major kinds of microorganisms—the protozoans, algae, fungi, bacteria, and viruses—it is the protozoans, the bacteria, and the viruses that are the chief agents of disease in higher animals. Only about 50 species of fungi (a relatively small number) cause deadly diseases in higher animals, and the algae do not seem to be responsible for any.

Fungal diseases come in two categories: superficial and systemic. The skin is the chief target for fungi that cause superficial diseases, because these organisms are able to grow on keratin, a substance found in skin, hair, and nails. The fungi cause itching and reddening of the skin. Ringworm of the scalp in children and athlete's foot in adults are typical superficial fungal ailments—not serious diseases, to be sure, but treatment is generally prolonged and not always successful, because very few

chemicals are effective against fungal infections. Systemic fungal disease often has symptoms resembling a mild cold. The fungi that cause the disease may eventually become distributed throughout the body; this results in a general weakening, but such disease is rarely deadly.

Protozoans, on the other hand, are at the root of a number of serious and possibly fatal ailments—for example, malaria, which is caused by any one of four species of the genus *Plasmodium*. These creatures have a complex life cycle, several stages of which take place in man, the others in mosquitoes of the genus *Anopheles*. When a person is bitten by an infected mosquito, small cells called *sporozoites* are injected into the bloodstream. These, the protozoan's infective units, are carried through the body until they reach and enter the cells of the liver. Here each sporozoite sets out to reproduce itself asexually by splitting in half. The resultant small cells, called *merozoites,* reenter the bloodstream, where they can infect the red blood corpuscles of the host, who becomes very ill as a result. The merozoites produce more of their kind within the red blood corpuscles, just as the sporozoites reproduce by division in the liver cells.

Not all the merozoites released from the red blood corpuscles are capable of infecting other corpuscles; some are capable of infecting only a mosquito. When an anopheles mosquito bites an infected man, it draws up these *gametocytes* (as the infective cells are called at this stage) with its ration of blood, and so they enter the mosquito's body. The mosquito may then bite another infected person, drawing up more gametocytes— this time, of course, from a completely different parent *Plasmodium*. Gametocytes from the two parents may then fuse, producing new creatures, which, by means of amoeboid movement, make their way to the mosquito's intestine. In the mosquito's gut, the amoebalike creatures grow and divide into a number of sporozoites. These in turn find their way to the salivary glands, where they become concentrated, available for transmission to a human being.

So the best way to prevent malaria is to wipe out the anopheles mosquito. Failing that, certain drugs such as quinine, paludrine, chloroquine, and atebrine are effective measures against the protozoan during its most virulent stage, when it is in the blood corpuscles.

Plasmodium and other protozoan parasites on higher animals may seem to us to lead rather

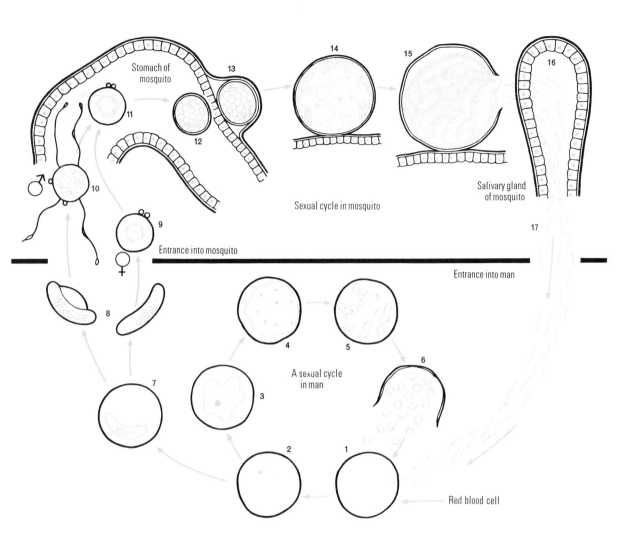

Stomach of mosquito

11

13

12

14

15

16

Sexual cycle in mosquito

Salivary gland of mosquito

17

Entrance into mosquito

Entrance into man

9

10

8

Red blood cell

A sexual cycle in man

7

3

2

1

4

5

6

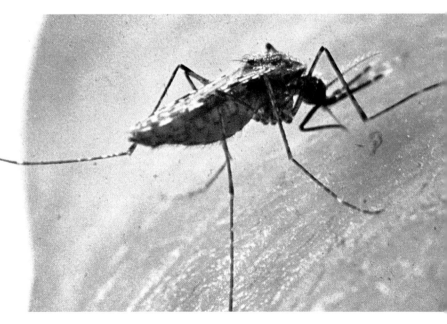

Anopheles *mosquito sucking blood from a human finger (right) also injects saliva that may contain* Plasmodium *protozoans—microorganisms that cause one of the world's chief debilitating and killing diseases: malaria. Mosquito and man play complementary roles in* Plasmodium's *complicated life cycle. Above:* Plasmodium *sporozoites entering man infect and destroy red blood cells and reproduce asexually (1–6), producing small cells called merozoites that give rise to sex cells called gametocytes (7–8). Sucked up with human blood into a mosquito's stomach, each female gametocyte becomes a mature macrogamete (9). Each male gametocyte produces microgametes (10). If one enters a macrogamete (11) the resulting oökinete (12) lodges in the outer stomach wall (13), becoming an oöcyst (14) that bursts, releasing sporozoites (15). Many reach the mosquito's salivary gland (16). These sporozoites can enter man (17).*

strange lives. But of all the weird life styles adopted by parasitic microorganisms, none is stranger than that of the viruses, as we have seen in our discussion of bacteriophages in Chapter 4. Although we have known about viruses since 1898, when two German scientists suggested that these tiny particles were responsible for foot-and-mouth disease in cattle, doctors have not yet learned how to control them. And so, because all viruses live as parasites in living creatures, it is just as well that most of them seem to coexist fairly harmlessly with their hosts. Why this should be so is not at all clear, but the fact remains that viral attack resulting in serious damage to the host is the exception rather than the rule. Furthermore, viruses that do great harm in one organism seem quite innocent in others. The encephalitic viruses, for example, are deadly to human beings but seem to live naturally and harmlessly in fowl.

Viruses have no means of locomotion and are transferred from one host to another only by wind, water, or personal contact. Similarly, they have no means of getting inside the host, but must depend on breaks in the skin (or in the roots, stems, or leaves of plants) or must enter through the mouth or lungs. But we really have little knowledge of precisely how a virus enters the body, whether of an animal or of a plant. And we have only a general idea of how it gets about once it is inside.

The target for the invading virus is an individual cell. Entry to a living cell, with its cell membrane, might seem an impossible task for a virus particle, which has neither teeth nor any other built-in tool for effecting an entrance (with the exception of the phages that parasitize bacteria). But the virus has an unusually subtle method of unlocking cell doors without breaking through the walls. Somehow it deceives the cell into taking it in as if it were food. How it manages the deception is not entirely clear, but entry evidently depends on the structure of both the virus and the cell membrane. If the viral key fits, the door opens and in goes the virus.

Once inside the cell, it takes over the cell's machinery for the construction of growth materials and redirects it into making new viral particles. Eventually, as for the phages, the newly created virus particles are released by the breakdown or bursting of the host cell. Such destruction on a large scale causes disease.

Viral diseases that afflict man include polio, encephalitis, influenza, and—most familiar of all ailments—the common cold. Because we have few ways of dealing with such diseases once infection has occurred, prevention rather than cure is the watchword. Immunization (the practice of using vaccine against viral attacks) is one such defense. Vaccines create artificial immunity to disease. When animals are attacked by hostile virus particles or bacterial cells, they produce antibodies whose function is to destroy the invaders. The process of immunization is based on the fact that once the antibodies for some diseases have been called forth, they circulate in the body and confer immunity against those diseases for quite a long time. So if a person is vaccinated—that is, artificially infected with a very mild dose of a disease—he builds up defenses against serious attacks.

Credit for discovering the value of vaccination is commonly given to an English doctor, Edward Jenner (1749–1823), who, although he did not really discover the process, found a way to make it safe. During a terrible epidemic of smallpox toward the end of the 18th century, Jenner noticed that farmers and milkmaids who had contracted the much less serious disease of cowpox seemed safe from smallpox, while those around them were dying in droves from the disease (which probably killed about 60 million people in various parts of the world during that century). Jenner wondered what would happen if he put some of the pus from a cowpox spot into

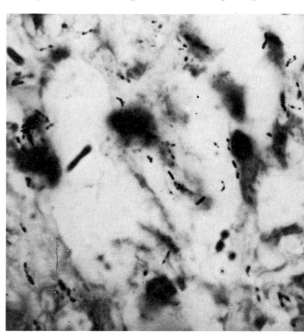

Hands reduced to stumps help to identify this Pakistani woman as a victim of the terrible and mildly infectious disease leprosy, caused by bacteria like those in the photomicrograph (left). Probably entering the body through breaks in the skin, rodlike Mycobacterium organisms multiply in skin and nerves and, if left untreated, sometimes cause bone damage that results in the loss of toes and fingers. Medicine is at last combating this disease, which affects millions of people in the tropics.

Edward Jenner's fight against smallpox.

Edward Jenner, the son of a clergyman, was born in 1749 at Berkeley, Gloucestershire. Although his family was not poor, Jenner became a surgeon's apprentice at the age of 13, because that was the best way to learn to be a doctor in those days.

YOU WERE BRAVE TO STAY WITH HE—DID YOU NOT FE INFECTION

ANOTHER DEATH FROM SMALLPOX—AND SHE WON'T BE THE LAST!

Bristol, in the 1760s...

POOR THING... I DID WHAT I COULD FOR HER.

NOT I, SI I'VE HAD COWPOX, CAN NEVE TAKE SMALLPO

...and Edward Jenner, a surgeon's apprentice, hears something he will never forge

Years later, as a successful doctor in the West Country, Jenner began to make a thorough study of *cowpox*.

AN INFECTION FROM THE UDDERS OF COWS. POSSIBLY A FORM OF SMALLPOX ITSELF—BUT MADE LESS DANGEROUS BY PASSING THROUGH SUCH A LARGE ANIMAL.

THE COWPOX BLISTERS ARE ALMOST EXACTLY LIKE THOSE OF SMALLPOX. I'M CERTAIN THAT OLD COUNT TALE IS TRUE — BUT NOW MUST PROVE THAT IT IS.

MOST OF US THAT HANDLES COWS CATCHES IT, SIR — LIKE MY MILKMAID HERE. HERE, SARAH, SHOW THE GENTLEMAN YOUR HANDS!

Jenner took fluid from one of the cowpox blisters on the hand of milkmaid Sarah Nelmes...

There was much opposition at first. Jenner was denounced as a quack by the "variolation" doctors—and jeered at by the ignorant.

ALL SOLDIERS WILL BE VACCINATED—BY ORDER OF 'IS 'IGHNESS THE DUKE O' YORK! YOU'LL EITHER 'AVE A LITTLE CUT FROM THE DOCTOR — OR A ROUND DOZEN WITH A CAT-O'-NINE-TAILS!

I... I DON'T LIKE THE LO O' THAT KN SERGEANT

NEW BROADSHEET —ONLY AN 'APENNY — READ ABOUT THE DOCTOR WHAT'S TRYIN' TO CHANGE FOLKS INTO COWS!

But recognition by members of the Royal Family, and by President Jefferson of America and Emperor Napoleon of France, helped to establish Jenner's discovery. In 1800...

COULD THAT BE TRUE, SIR? WHAT THE GIRL SAID...?

IT'S AN OLD BELIEF OF OUR COUNTRYFOLK, EDWARD. WISH IT WERE TRUE. SMALLPOX KILLS NIGH 40,000 IN ENGLAND EVERY YEAR & LEAVES MANY MORE DISFIGURED, DEAF OR BLIND.

In years when it was at its height, smallpox sometimes accounted for *one death in every five*. There was little protection: "variolation"— deliberately infecting a patient with a "mild" form of smallpox—had been introduced from the East in 1713. Some unscrupulous doctors made a fortune from practicing it. . . .

Patients sometimes died from the treatment—and they were even more dangerous as a source of infection to others!

CHEAP AT TEN GUINEAS! A SHORT ILLNESS & THEN YOU'LL NEVER FEAR SMALLPOX AGAIN...

...SO LONG AS YOU SURVIVE!

James did not develop smallpox—and in 1798, after more experiments had been successful, including one on his own baby son, Jenner published his findings.

. . . and rubbed it into two small cuts made on the arm of eight-year-old James Phipps. James developed cowpox. Six weeks later, on 14 May 1796, James had recovered from cowpox—and Jenner made his great experiment.

THE COWPOX MADE ME POORLY FOR A FEW DAYS, DOCTOR. WILL THIS DO THE SAME?

AYE, JAMES...

...AND PRAY HEAVEN I'M RIGHT & IT WILL DO NO MORE — FOR THIS IS SMALLPOX!

THE ROYAL SOCIETY REFUSED TO ACCEPT MY RESEARCH — BUT IF I PUBLISH IT MYSELF IMPORTANT PEOPLE ARE BOUND TO READ IT. THEY MUST BE MADE TO BELIEVE THAT 'VACCINATION' WORKS!

AN INQUIRY INTO CAUSE AND EFFECTS OF THE VARIOLAE VACCINAE

Jenner's method was called from *vacca*, the Latin word fluid from smallpox blisters "vaccine."

"vaccination" for "cow." The that he used was called

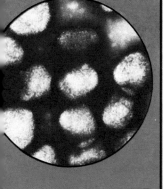

The mild infection of cowpox caused the patient's body to produce "antibodies" that protected it against the deadly smallpox. But although reasonably efficient microscopes existed in his time, Jenner probably never saw the microorganisms of the smallpox virus . . .

Between 1800 and 1900, deaths in England from smallpox fell by about 95 per cent. Vaccination was made compulsory in 1853, and became voluntary in 1948.

a cut made on the arm of a healthy child; he tried the experiment, and the boy caught cowpox. Later on, in a clinching experiment, he inoculated the same boy with pus from a smallpox spot. After a few anxious days, it became clear that the boy had achieved immunity from smallpox. What had happened was that the cowpox virus, which is very similar to the smallpox virus, had called forth antibodies that provided protection against both diseases.

These days, the virus particles used for immunization against diseases such as smallpox, poliomyelitis, and measles are cultured especially to be effective at causing the body to produce antibodies but without causing the disease proper. These so-called *attenuated* particles are effective because it is the specific chemical content of the virus, not its ability to reproduce, that is the important factor in calling forth the antibodies.

If immunization is not used, or if it fails, there is little that doctors can do about a virus disease except let it run its course. Such antibiotics as penicillin, which are remarkably effective against bacteria, are not much use for controlling viruses; at best, they can merely help to moderate a viral attack. Fortunately, the body produces not only specific antibodies against specific viruses, but also a more general weapon in the form of defense substances called *interferons*. These are called forth whenever the cells are invaded by viruses, and they stop the viral particles from multiplying. Interferons are different from antibodies in that they do not combat a specific invader. Once initiated, they prevent the multiplication of any virus that attacks.

Like the viruses, bacteria must gain access to their victims without the help of teeth, claws, or any other organs specialized for breaking and entering, and they too are spread from one individual to another either through the air, by personal contact, or through infected food or drink. They do not always survive the trip, for if they cannot live on the skin surface, they will die unless they can make their way inside through a body orifice or a break in the skin. Once inside, however, they grow and multiply, frequently close to the point of entrance. If they get into the bloodstream, they may be distributed throughout the body and begin to grow in all the tissues that they reach, although it is more usual for a particular bacterium to grow only in a specific tissue.

Brucella abortus, a spherical bacterium that causes contagious abortion in cattle, concentrates in the unborn offspring and maternal fluids of the pregnant cow, and abortion results in about four out of every 10 cases. This same bacterium can also infect human beings, but without injuring the fetus; instead it causes undulant fever, characterized by chills and a fever that increases at night and drops during the day. Apparently the embryonic tissues of a cow contain a chemical that stimulates the growth of these bacteria. But people do not contain this substance, and so the bacteria becomes widely distributed instead of concentrating on a specific tissue.

The most specialized form of bacterial transmission through bodily contact is found in the highly contagious venereal diseases, gonorrhea and syphilis. Syphilis, the more virulent of these two social scourges, is caused by an unusual type of bacterium, one of the spirochete family. The spirochetes are slender, spiral-shaped cells, which may be of quite considerable length. They move with a snakelike motion as the spiral cell alternately contracts and relaxes—a unique form of locomotion in the microbial world. Gonorrhea bacteria cause local inflammation of the urinary and genital organs, but rarely produce serious complications or death. Syphilis bacteria, on the other hand, may spread from these sites to other parts of the body and may cause damage to the central nervous system, producing paralysis and insanity. Both these types of bacterium, however, are easily killed by adverse conditions. They cannot survive desiccation, extreme changes of temperature, or strong ultraviolet light. In fact, they are so sensitive to heat that, before the advent of antibiotics, doctors used to treat syphilis by raising the temperature of the patient's body—perhaps by inducing a fever artificially—in order to kill off the spirochetes.

Various other bacteria damage their unwilling hosts in a number of ways. Sometimes—though rarely—they do great harm just by sheer weight of numbers. A large mass of cells can block veins, arteries, or the valves of the heart, or they can clog the air passages in the lungs. But they are more likely to bring on diseases through the production of poisonous substances. The bacterium that causes diphtheria, a club-shaped microorganism that lives in the respiratory tract, is of historical interest because it was the first bacterium to be recognized by scientists as a

MERCVRE.

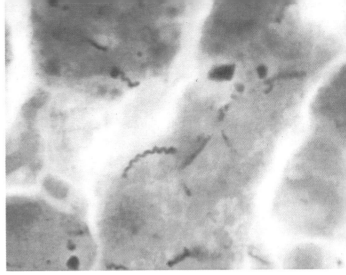

Courtship *(below) may lead to sexual union in which a partner with venereal disease can unwittingly transmit the disease bacteria to the other partner. The spirochete bacterium* Treponema pallidum *(photomicrograph, above) causes syphilis, worst of all venereal diseases. Old "cures" included taking mercury (woodcut, left), but penicillin is the modern treatment.*

poison-producer. The poison is an excretory product, and it can be as unfortunate for the bacterium as for the victim, because the microbe is unlikely to survive the death of its host.

Bacterial poisons can damage virtually any part of the body. Some, for example, attack the nervous system. One such poison causes tetanus by attaching itself to the point where one nerve fiber makes contact with another. The result is that the message being passed between nerves is hindered or canceled, with consequent paralysis in the affected muscles.

All the many instances of how man and other animals can be attacked, invaded, and in some cases killed by parasitic microorganisms might lead you to believe that the higher animals are sitting targets for microbial disaster. Fortunately, this is far from true. In addition to production of antibodies and interferons—or, as biologists call these defense mechanisms, "the immune response"—at least two powerful natural defense systems are always at work in our bodies. The first is the presence of *phagocytes*—a name meaning literally "cells that eat." And this is just what these cells, which resemble amoebas, do: they seek out, engulf, and swallow menacing alien cells. They reside in the bone marrow and in the bloodstream, where they are popularly known as "white corpuscles," and their numbers increase enormously during an infection. When a bacterium has been engulfed by a phagocyte, the cell's digestive juices swiftly destroy the microbe. It is interesting to note that practice makes perfect with these hunter cells. Once a phagocyte has swallowed its first invader, it becomes about 10 times more effective at tackling the next alien particle of the same type.

This is a very effective scavenging system. From 80 to 90 per cent of all foreign particles that enter the liver in the blood, for example, are removed by the phagocytes at one sweep. In the end, though, aggressive bacteria occasionally overcome these steadfast warriors.

The second line of defense is inflammation. Increased blood flow to an affected region of the body causes the tissues to swell, with accompanying heat and pain. The swollen tissues are likely to produce blood clots, which can then trap the invading bacteria in their meshes, making it easier for phagocytes to pick off the invaders.

As we all know, however, no defense is foolproof. The immune response is the most specific—and in many ways the most effective—protection against microbial invasion; yet the amazing flexibility of microorganisms enables them sometimes to circumvent even this obstacle. Some bacteria, for example, coat themselves in an outer layer of material that resembles the victim's own proteins. Because the body releases antibodies only when threatened by alien proteins, it does not react against such a camouflaged intruder, and so the bacterium makes its entrance under false colors. For example, *Streptococcus pyogenes*—which can cause a number of diseases in man, ranging from a sore throat to pneumonia and rheumatic fever—often escapes pursuit because it is coated in a chemical common in human connective tissue.

Not all diseases are caused by microorganisms; some are inherited, and others may come as a result of poor diet, a rigorous environment, nervous strain, or a number of other disabilities. And the microorganism is only one factor in the disease with which it is associated. We have seen something of the balance between the weapons of the invader and the defenses of the host. The microorganism may be a necessary cause, but it is not sufficient in itself. For infection to take place, the host must be susceptible, and not all hosts are equally sensitive to microbial attack. The health of the host, the vigor of the microorganism, and the presence or absence of specific immunity all contribute to the outcome of infection. In an infectious disease, potential victim and microorganism interact.

It is easy to believe that because some of the invisible creatures cause disease, all of them are harmful to man. Not only is this not true, but it is actually *very* wide of the mark. Most microorganisms are either harmless or beneficial to man, whether directly or indirectly. Much of the world's food depends on the nitrogen-fixing activities of microorganisms, and their activities in the digestive systems of cows and sheep play a massive part in helping to nourish and clothe us. As we shall see in the next chapter, the tiny creatures also confer other benefits upon us. And so, even while acknowledging the damage that some microbes do, we should not forget that the other side of the picture is very bright indeed.

In this photomicrograph an amoebalike macrophage (a phago-cytic cell) is engulfing a carbon particle that has accidentally entered a lung. Macrophages acting as police and street cleaners are part of the body's first line of defense against invading, hostile microorganisms and other foreign bodies.

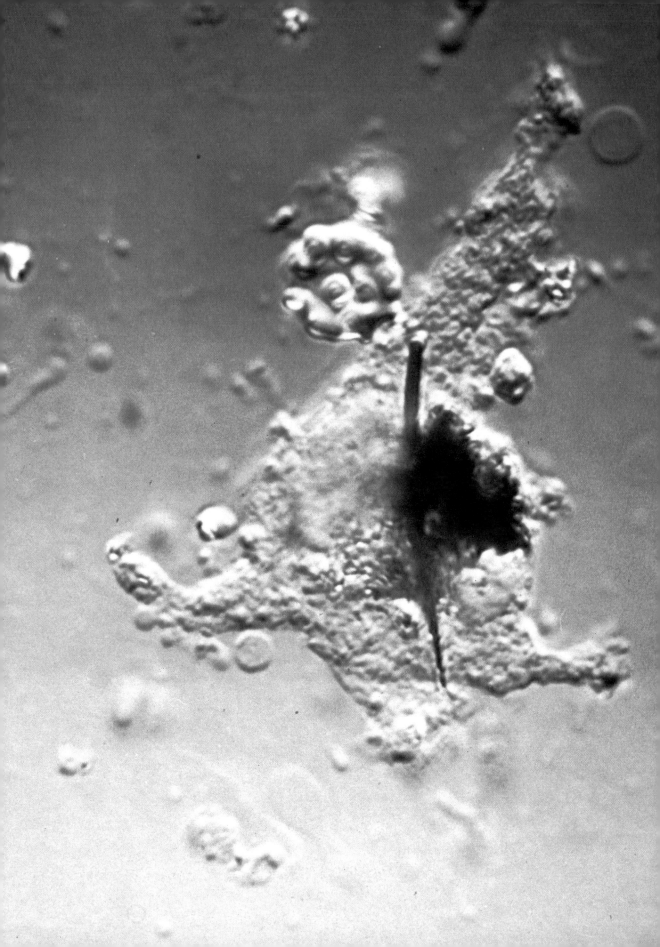

Destroyers and Creators

Biodeterioration and *biodegradation* are the fearsome names that modern scientists give to two aspects of microbial life that man has been familiar with ever since building his first primitive shelter and tasting his first alcoholic drink. *Biodeterioration* is a term that covers all the many different ways in which microorganisms (and some larger creatures as well) are able to attack and damage materials, whether mountains or masonry, fish cakes or fuel lines. *Biodegradation* includes all the processes through which living creatures break down waste matter, or convert complex substances into simpler ones.

As so often where microorganisms are concerned, there are both benefits and disadvantages for man in these activities. On the one hand, the overall cost of preventing microbial damage to food and fabric, and of repairing the damage where prevention has failed, is astronomical. On the other hand, without the unwitting help of microorganisms there would be no cheese, yogurt, beer, or wine, and the disposal of waste and refuse would be an even greater problem than it is. Moreover, many of the minute creatures whose insatiable appetites can destroy living human flesh are themselves susceptible to attack by other members of their invisible world. And so, in the use of antibiotics, for example, we have learned how to use their capacity for doing damage to one another as a weapon against those that do damage to us.

Antibiotics, which are chemical substances produced naturally by some fungi and other microorganisms, were discovered by the Scottish bacteriologist Sir Alexander Fleming less than half a century ago. In 1928, while growing cells of the bacterium *Staphylococcus* in his laboratory, Fleming noticed that one of his preparations had become contaminated by a mold-producing

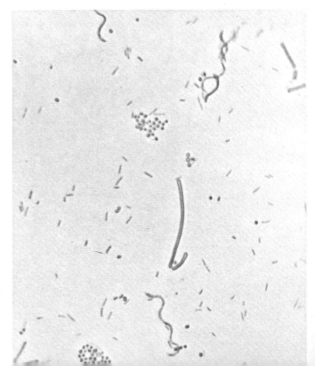

Dots and squiggles (right) are wall-grown bacteria, much enlarged. Such tiny, harmless-seeming organisms flourishing on stone in damp air produce acids that can help rot a city. Eroded statue of an angel (above) and crumbling canal-front buildings (far right) reveal the decay that threatens Venice.

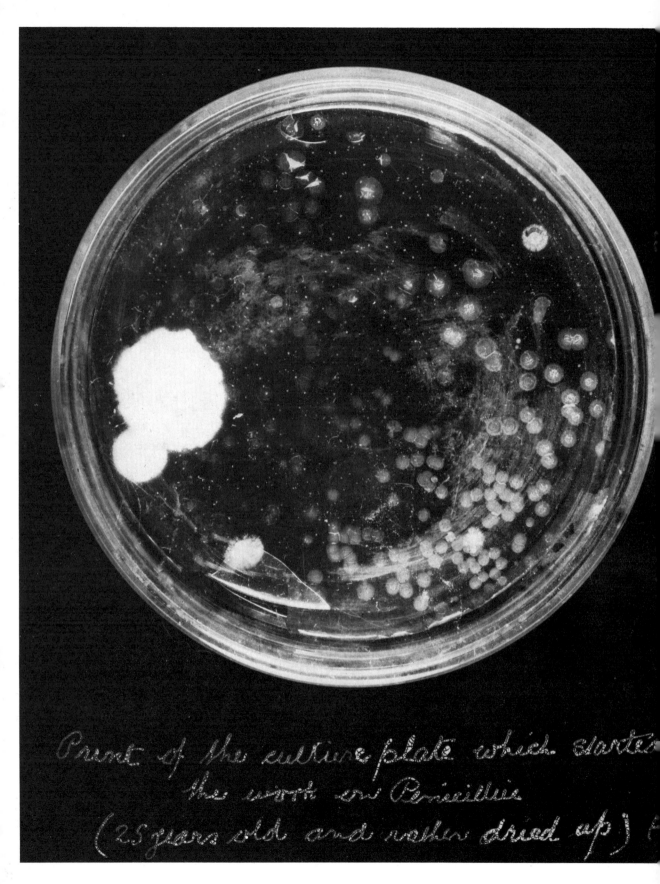

Print of the culture plate which starter
the work on Penicillin
(25 years old and rather dried up)

fungus. He also observed that the area around the fungus was entirely free of living bacteria. From this observation and subsequent experiments, Fleming discovered that the intrusive fungus was manufacturing a substance that prevented the growth of the bacteria. Because the fungus was identifiable as *Penicillium,* he gave the name *penicillin* to the substance.

Penicillin was only the first of many antibiotics. We know very little about how they work when introduced into diseased tissue, but we do know that these microorganism-produced substances have a lethal effect upon other microorganisms (chiefly, though not exclusively, bacteria). Some of them seem to prevent bacteria from manufacturing their cell walls; others kill the bacterial cell membrane; still others inhibit bacterial protein synthesis. We understand almost nothing about the role of antibiotics in nature. Some scientists believe that they are actively involved in the competition among rival microbes for living space and food — but it also seems possible that only microorganisms grown in the laboratory produce such boons to modern medicine as penicillin and streptomycin. At any rate, they *are* boons. And they compensate, at least partly, for the havoc wrought by other forms of microbial life.

Because of the apparently endless variety of ways in which microorganisms get the energy that they need for life, they are able to use — in other words, to damage — virtually anything. Most living creatures get their energy only from the breakdown of sugars, protein, and fats, but microbes can survive on such foodstuffs as metal, paper, or paint. There are bacteria able to live on iron, and they can reduce iron and steel pipes to crumbling shells. And there are bacteria and fungi that eat the rubber insulating layer around the metal core of electric cables. So great is this problem that where a cable is to be laid in a particularly exposed position, a fungicide — a chemical that kills fungi — may be incorporated into the rubber of the sheath.

What might seem, at first glance, a bizarre example of the way microorganisms are able to feed on unlikely materials is to be found in the huge tanks used for bulk storage of fuels, especially petroleum and kerosine. When these tanks are filled, it is impossible to prevent some moisture from entering with the fuel. This eventually separates out as a layer of water under the fuel (for water is the denser of the two liquids), and bacteria and fungi grow in great numbers where the fuel and water are in contact. This is, in fact, not surprising. Petroleum is a rich source for the kinds of chemical on which these microorganisms live; after all, the production of petroleum was partly the work of long-dead microorganisms, and everyone knows that petroleum is a source of energy.

Oil-eating microbes have become a severe hazard in jet-airplane fuel systems, which burn kerosine. If microorganisms get into the kerosine, the fuel filters become clogged with microbial debris, with resultant power loss; furthermore, microbes growing in an aircraft's fuel tanks can cause corrosion. To minimize such dangers, the kerosine is strained through special filters, and chemicals that prevent the growth of bacteria and fungi are added to it. In addition, the inner walls of the fuel tanks are coated with a plastic substance that is resistant to attack by microorganisms, and the tanks are washed out at regular intervals with a lethal substance.

It is not surprising that microorganisms devour wood, but it may be surprising to learn that they also damage stone. Indeed, in attacking the surface of exposed rock faces and boulders, they often break off tiny particles, which constitute the first stage in soil formation. They also threaten the structure of stone buildings and contribute to the gradual wearing down of old statues and carvings.

How do such miniscule creatures manage to damage great rocks? If you examine almost any large area of exposed stone, you will find algae and lichens either lying dormant in dry weather or growing profusely in wet weather. The foods that they produce through photosynthesis also support the growth of other microorganisms, such as bacteria and fungi. All these single-celled organisms breathe in oxygen and give out carbon dioxide gas, and as the carbon dioxide dissolves in the surrounding moisture, it forms carbonic acid. This, together with other acids produced naturally by the microorganisms, helps to dissolve the surface of the rock, causing small particles to break away.

The culture plate on which Fleming first noticed Penicillium *mold spreading and curbing the growth of* Staphylococcus *bacteria. The big double blob is the* Penicillium. *Smaller blobs are* Staphylococcus *colonies. Between the two is an area where penicillin produced by the mold has caused the bacteria colonies to begin to break up. (This photograph was taken when the culture was 25 years old and rather dried up.)*

Meanwhile, the cracks and fissures in the rock that result from freezing and thawing gradually become filled with soil, which allows the growth not merely of larger plants but of further colonies of microbes. And so the deterioration caused by the combined efforts of weather, microorganisms, and larger plants progresses.

Even road surfaces deteriorate because of bacterial growth on substances present in asphalt and bitumen. And among other materials that you might wrongly assume to be impervious to attack is the glass of lenses and mirrors. The glass itself is not eaten by microorganisms. What happens is that tiny amounts of it are damaged by the acids that they produce, but the minor destruction is enough to spoil delicate optical surfaces. In the tropics especially, certain types of fungus grow on the dust around lenses or on the adhesives used in mounting the lenses in cameras and binoculars, or on the special substances that coat lens surfaces. The fungal acids etch the glass, and even the use of fungicides and meticulous efforts to keep surfaces dry and dust-free will not always protect them from invasion.

Paints, too, are subject to various forms of biodegradation. Fungi growing on the timber to which paints are applied may discolor them, or they can be damaged by fungi in the dust on the paint surface. There is a quite common bacterium that goes to work on paint as it is being used, and other kinds of bacteria often thrive inside stored tins of paint.

In fact, there seems to be only one kind of material substance that comes close to defeating the microbes: man-made plastics. There are some bacteria that attack plastics, including polyethylene—but it is slow going for them, and they do not get far. As we have seen, microorganisms can break down virtually every other substance, returning the chemicals from which it is made to the soil, sea, or air. But plastics are a remarkable exception to the rule. It has been suggested that as archaeologists of the future dig their way down through the layers of debris left by successive civilizations, they will be able to recognize ours instantly because our remains will be composed chiefly of discarded plastic wrappers, bottles, cups, bags, and other such indestructible items.

The reason why the microbes are so baffled by plastics is that they must, like any other form of life, obey the rules of chemistry. They can degrade materials only if they are able to produce chemical substances that can act upon the material to be degraded. No microorganism had ever confronted a man-made plastic before the early part of this century, and so none had ever evolved chemicals to deal with such an unnatural material. No doubt the inexorable force of the evolutionary process will eventually produce a microbe that can change a plastic bag into a fine dinner. In the meantime, modern science is doing what it can to help solve the problem.

For it *is* a problem, and an oddly paradoxical one: while science searches for new and better ways to protect materials against microbial attack, science also searches for ways to make one kind of material vulnerable to the microbes. Unless either natural evolution or science comes to our rescue, the modern world is in danger of burying itself under a mountain of non-biodegradable plastics!

The scientists' efforts have recently met with some success. The British, for example, are working on the development of a plastic that would disintegrate when exposed to direct sunlight. Polyethylene, polypropylene, and other commercial plastics could then be manufactured in such a way that wrappers and containers made from such substances would remain usable in diffuse daylight, and even in sunlight filtered through a window pane; but exposure to direct sunlight would initiate a process of disintegration leading to the formation of a harmless granular substance, which would be composed of chemicals that bacteria could recognize and break down. By adjusting the amounts of the various constituents of the new plastics, its makers could probably vary its outdoor lifetime from about three months to five years.

Apart from plastics, however, practically all materials provide both habitats and food for the invisible marauders. And some of the destruction that they wreak on substances of value to man are actually tragic. Among the most serious kinds of microbiological deterioration—to us, at any rate—is the spoilage of foodstuffs. What this costs economically is impossible to estimate accurately, but the global figure must be billions of dollars annually.

We describe food as "spoiled" when it is no longer attractive or safe to eat. The loss is due not to the amount of food that the microorganisms take (although, given time, they will

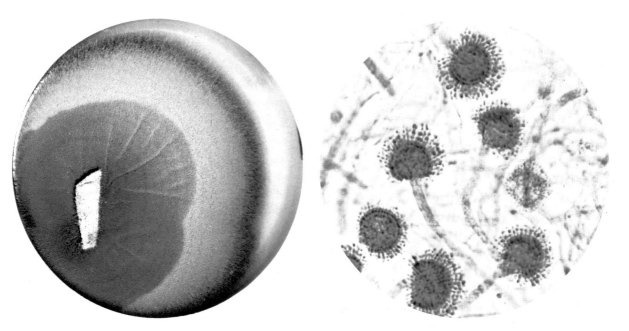

Three fungi that harm products of modern technology. Above left: Cladosporium resinae *culture growing on an aircraft filter. This fungus corrodes the interiors of water-contaminated metal fuel tanks. Above right: photomicrograph of an* Aspergillus *fungus. Members of this genus erode optical lenses. Below: here a frothy mold feasts on insulation material sheathing an electric cable.*

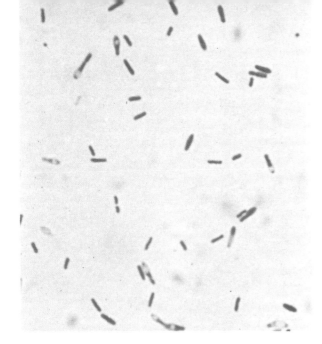

completely consume a whole carcass or an entire field of grain) but to the substances they produce while feeding.

These chemical by-products of the feeding process may render the food completely unfit for human consumption simply by making it taste or smell foul. In many cases the smell and taste are all that makes the food unattractive, for it is still perfectly safe to eat. In other cases, however, microorganisms produce poisonous substances that can cause serious or even fatal diseases. A classical example of such a disease is the bacteria-generated botulin poisoning that we discussed in an earlier chapter.

Microorganisms are present in such large numbers in the air, soil, and water, as well as on the skin and in the bodies of man and other mammals, that it is extremely difficult to prevent food from becoming contaminated, especially if it has to be kept for any length of time before being eaten. For example, the flesh of cattle butchered for beef probably contains very few microorganisms; but the skin and intestines are sure to be highly contaminated, and the

Germs rot or poison food exposed at normal temperatures. Rod-shaped Clostridium botulinum *(above, enlarged 500 times) breeds in badly canned food and the food can kill if swallowed. But efficient canning prevents bacterial growth. Food abandoned in Antarctica by Scott's last expedition (photographed below and right) thus proved sound after years in the Southern Hemisphere's great polar icebox.*

contaminating organisms will in turn contaminate workers in abattoirs. The workers and their instruments will then pass the microbes on to the flesh. Furthermore, if an animal is inefficiently killed, its heart may continue to beat for a time. In such an event, any organisms that manage to gain access to the bloodstream through open wounds will be swept around the body as the blood circulates.

Fortunately, the standard of cleanliness in most modern abattoirs is high, and freshly slaughtered flesh is quickly chilled to prevent the growth of all but a few bacteria. Cooking provides the final deathblow for these bacteria, which cannot survive high temperatures. Real danger arises only when meat is allowed to stand for some time at temperatures that permit the growth of microorganisms.

Food spoilage is so much a part of our common heritage that the words used to describe the different sorts of stale food are more folksy than scientific. Thus we traditionally talk of moldiness and "whiskers" when foods become covered with spots of fungus, "sliminess" when the surface of meat or fish is damaged by bacteria, and "ropiness" when bacteria cause a sticky material to form in wine, vinegar, or milk. In this century, however, some new terms have been added to the food-spoilage vocabulary because certain forms of spoilage have become possible only through the advent of modern food technology, especially canning. Although canning is a technique used specifically to preserve food from microbial attack, the technique itself involves risks. "Flat sours" is the odd name given to spoilage caused in canned foods by organisms that ferment the food without producing gases as a by-product. "Blown cans" describes what happens when another kind of bacteria ferments food inside cans, but this time *with* the production of gas: the gas distends and distorts the walls and ends of the can and may eventually blow it open.

The contamination that results in such spoilage as "flat sours" or "blown cans" happens infrequently as a consequence of some sort of error in the canning process, but it does happen, and it can sometimes have tragic or near-tragic

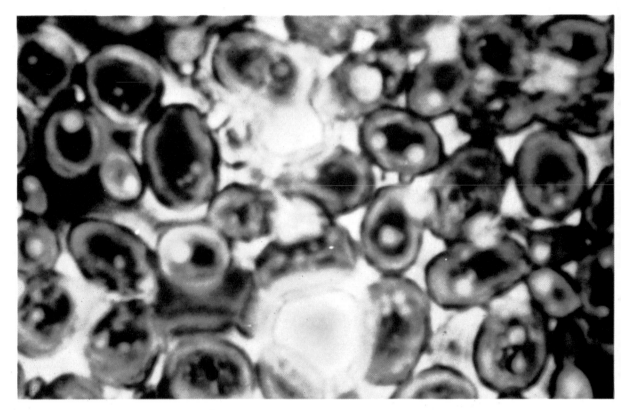

Photomicrograph of yeast cells growing on gas oil. The resulting crop is concentrated, dried, and purified, and the end product is a protein used to feed farm livestock. In such ways, microorganisms may help combat a mounting world food shortage.

Right: salmon hanging in a Suffolk smokehouse in eastern England. Warm smoke from hardwood sawdust dries the fish and impregnates it with chemicals including wood creosote. This process confers flavor and protection against decay bacteria.

results. Some years ago, cases of typhoid broke out in areas where people had eaten canned corned beef from Argentina. The faulty cans had been cooled in Plata River water after an improper sealing, and poisonous *Salmonella* bacteria, which abound in the river, had entered the cans and multiplied in the meat.

Some foodstuffs can be contaminated with harmful microorganisms in their raw state. For instance, the eggs of hens and ducks can be infected by *Salmonella* bacteria, which have been known to attach themselves to the outside of the shell, penetrate it, and grow inside. But this sort of attack is fortunately rare, and so food scientists are chiefly concerned with the problem of maintaining the quality of meat or of plant produce in the period between the death of the animal or the gathering of the crop and its consumption. In the tropics, where warmth and humidity are conducive to the swift growth of bacteria, decay takes place very quickly indeed. This explains the traditional use of curry powders, herbs, and spices in hot countries;

such strong seasoning masks the unpleasant odor and taste of decaying but usually harmless food.

Nowadays we have a number of different ways to prevent—or at least delay—spoilage. The first is refrigeration, which, although it does not kill bacteria, slows down the rate at which they can grow and reproduce themselves. When food is kept frozen at very low temperatures it can be stored almost indefinitely, for frozen microorganisms remain totally inactive. Supplies left in the Antarctic by the ill-fated Scott expedition in 1912 were discovered many years later in perfect condition. And mammoths that died and became embedded in the Siberian ice fields many thousands of years ago have been disinterred with their flesh still edible.

At the other end of the temperature scale, food is also preserved by great heat. Canning and bottling, for example, work on the principle of killing bacteria already present and ensuring that no others can get in. To do this, the food is thoroughly cooked, then placed in sterilized cans or bottles and reheated under pressure, and

the containers are sealed while still very hot. This is a useful technique, but it must be strictly controlled or it can go wrong.

Pasteurization, named for its inventor, Louis Pasteur (1822–95), is a heating technique for preserving milk and other fluids. Two general methods are in use today. The traditional way of pasteurizing milk involves heating the liquid to about 160°F for 15 seconds, then cooling it quickly to about 54°F and pouring it into sterilized bottles, which are capped immediately. This is called "flash pasteurization." In a more recent modification of this technique, the fluid is held at 150°F for 30 minutes before being cooled. But an entirely different—and much newer—method of preserving milk is to heat the liquid to an extremely high temperature— about 270°F—for one second and then instantly seal it into containers. This is how modern long-lasting milk is treated so as to remain "fresh" for months. The very high temperature kills many more of the contaminating microorganisms than does traditional pasteurization, though it does cause the milk to have a different flavor.

Food may also be preserved by drying it or by immersing it in high concentrations of sugar or salt. Bacteria cannot live without moisture, and in highly concentrated solutions the water is drawn out of them. More modern techniques involve the use of such chemicals as sulfur dioxide, proprionic acid, and sodium nitrate. These are *bacteriostatic*—that is, they prevent microorganisms from multiplying in food, but do not kill them. Very small amounts of these preservatives are used, because large doses of them can be dangerous to human beings.

Pickling food in vinegar and the smoking of meats and fish are also examples of chemical preservation, although most of the people who have been pickling and smoking their foods for many generations have hardly been aware of that fact. Vinegar, of course, is a weak acid, and acids either kill bacteria or control their growth. As for smoking, the special flavour that it adds to certain kinds of food is only one of its virtues; the other is that the smoke impregnates the surface of the food with microbe-inhibiting chemicals. Combined with the heat of the process, the effects of the smoke enormously reduce the number of bacteria in a piece of fish or meat.

To pass from the most old-fashioned to the most newfangled of preservation techniques is to move into our age of controlled radio-activity. Because bacteria are killed by ultraviolet light, which is a natural constituent of sunlight, we now sterilize all sorts of things by means of radiation. You may have noticed that electric razors for general use in airports and other public places are often enclosed in boxes filled with blue light. This is ultraviolet light, used to kill "germs" that might otherwise be transferred from one person to another. Ultraviolet light cannot penetrate very far into foods, though. So we use a much stronger kind of radiation as a preservative. The food is first sealed into a container, and then exposed to radiation from a radioactive cobalt source. Because the cobalt never comes near it, the food itself is not contaminated with radioactivity, but the radiation that passes through the packaging and the food kills all microorganisms. Any edible matter treated in this fashion really does become completely sterile.

Some foods, however, are *improved* by being infected. Best steak, for example, benefits from "hanging" for a certain time, because the by-product of bacterial activity is a steak that is more tender and tasty. It must not hang too long, though, or the good taste will turn bad. But the wide range of natural dairy products is a familiar example of good-to-eat infected food.

Untreated raw milk quickly goes "bad," of course. This is because it is attacked by various species of bacterium that convert milk sugar into an acid that sours it. Yeasts and other fungi can live on this acid. Then, when they have used it up, bacteria—whose growth has so far been inhibited by the acid—take over and degrade the milk proteins, while still other microorganisms degrade the milk fats. And so the soured milk turns rancid—unless some or all of these processes of biodegradation are taken advantage of for the production of such foods as butter, cheese, yogurt, buttermilk, sour cream, acidophilus milk, Icelandic *skyr,* and exotic intoxicating beverages such as kefir and koumiss, which come from southern Russia.

The dairy industry today is big business, and old-style hit-or-miss methods of producing milk products have given way to precise techniques, which make such production possible on a large scale. Butter, for example, is made from milk fat—that is, the cream—acted upon by two different sorts of organism. Nowadays, after the cream has been pasteurized, a special "starter culture" of the right bacteria is used in order

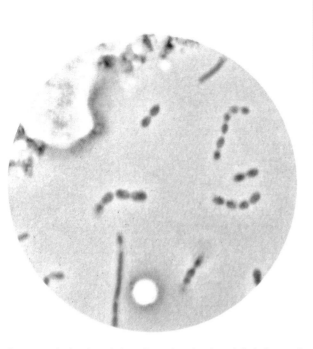

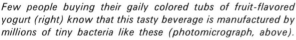

Few people buying their gaily colored tubs of fruit-flavored yogurt (right) know that this tasty beverage is manufactured by millions of tiny bacteria like these (photomicrograph, above).

to get the process going. In the old days, however, when time and mass production were less demanding than they are now, microbes floating in naturally from the atmosphere would have done the job.

Yogurt is started in a rather similar way. Even on a very small scale, it pays to use a starter culture; and, in fact, a little of the preceding batch of yogurt is often used as such a culture for each successive batch. The starter is added to pasteurized milk. When this is incubated at about 95°F, the microorganisms produce acids by fermenting the milk sugar. These acids coagulate proteins in the milk, and there you have it: yogurt. Kefir, koumiss, and other fermented milk products are all produced in basically the same way, but tastes and the available raw materials vary.

The end-product—whether liquid or solid, fizzy or alcoholic, thick or thin—depends on the kind of milk, the types of microorganism that go to work on it, the permitted degree of fermentation, and so on. "Fermentation," incidentally, is a word that we use mainly when referring to the decomposition of such organic substances as sugars and other carbohydrates. The chemical breakdown of proteins by the microorganisms is called "putrefaction."

Bacteria play a major role in the development of acidity and specific flavors in cheese. A basic cheese is made, quite simply, by curdling milk with rennin, an enzyme that coagulates it. This coagulated milk—or cheese, as it has become—is stored; and during its period in storage, the flavor and aroma develop as a result of the slow growth of certain types of microorganism within it. Cheeses of the Cheddar, Cheshire, and Wensleydale varieties are said to be "bacterially" ripened, and need no further microorganisms added during the storage period. But others, such as Camembert and Brie, are encouraged to grow mold on their outer surfaces. And some—Stilton and Danish Blue, for instance—are pierced with long rods to allow mold spores to reach the inside of the cheese. Some of the invisible organisms that flourish in cheese produce gases as a result of the fermentation process; and the gases, trapped and with no outlet, forcibly open spaces within the cheese. Thus are formed the holes in such varieties of cheese as Gruyère and Emmental.

The other universally known and enjoyed product of microbial fermentation is bread, which owes its several characteristic textures and flavors to various species of *Saccharomyces*, a minute fungus commonly called *yeast*. When yeast is added to flour-and-water dough, it leavens the mixture—which means that the fungi ferment the sugars that are in the dough and thus produce carbon dioxide gas. This makes

Each cheese on these pages appears below a photomicrograph revealing something of microorganisms found in it. Different microbes help to produce different cheeses. Bacteria known as streptococci *and* lactobacilli *ripen English Cheddar (above).*

Mold-ripened cheeses include Brie, a soft French cheese from the plateau east of Paris, and a close relative of Camembert. With such cheeses, a surface smear of Penicillium *mold forms a white film and softens the cheese from the outside inward.*

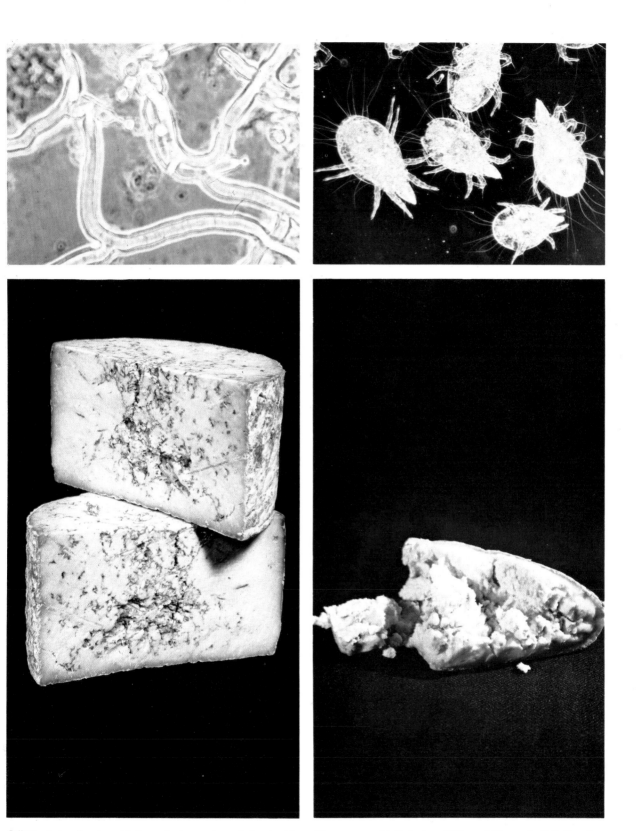

Stilton, a semihard mold-ripened cheese from Leicestershire and Derbyshire in England, gets its bluish interior veining from Penicillium roquefortii. *This mold grows in crannies inside the cheese. Molds, yeasts, and bacteria thrive on the crust.*

The same mold that gives Stilton yields semisoft Italian Gorgonzola. But not all tiny organisms in cheese are equally beneficial to us. The cheese mites in the photomicrograph above do nothing to create cheese: instead, they avidly devour it.

131

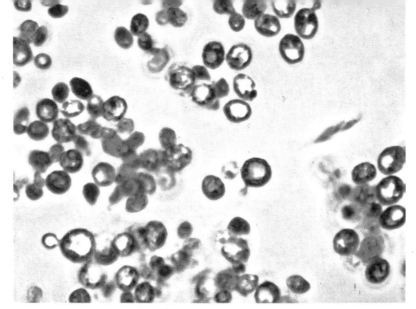

Bread-making exploits yeast's ability to breed explosively. Left: asymmetrical "dumbbells" (shown much enlarged) are Saccharomyces yeast cells multiplying. Each baby simply buds off from a single parent. The growing cells produce chemical agents that convert the starch in dough to sugar and the sugar to alcohol and carbon dioxide gas. Gas bubbles make the dough rise. Yeast breeds so fast that a mere pinch doubles the size of a lump of dough in two hours. After fermentation comes baking. This kills the yeast cells and causes alcohol to evaporate. Below: shoveling finished loaves from a baker's oven in France.

the dough less dense and increases its volume.

The fungi also add a "yeasty" flavor to the mixture. This is splendid as long as it remains within bounds, but if the taste of yeast becomes too strong, the flavor loses its delicate appeal. Thus the objective in bread-making is to permit the yeast to produce just the right amount of gas, for too many yeast cells spoil not only the taste but also the consistency of the loaf. This is why bread must be popped into the oven at just the right moment; the extreme heat of cooking kills the yeast cells.

Considering how much bread is baked and eaten in the world, it is not surprising that yeast is grown on an industrial scale these days. It is nurtured in fermentors—huge steel vessels ranging in capacity from 5000 to 15,000 gallons. A 15,000-gallon fermentor can be as high as a three-story building. The yeast cells in the fermentor are nourished on molasses and a number of other substances that cause them to multiply fast, but without producing much of the carbon dioxide gas that a baker expects when he adds them to his dough. In 12 hours inside a warm well-aerated fermentor, the number of yeast cells increases five-fold. At regular intervals some of them are removed from the fermentor and molded into blocks, which are then stored under refrigeration.

Dried yeast, which you can buy from your local store, is in reality nothing but a vast collection of spores, which will germinate to yield free-living yeast cells only if you place them in a suitable environment, such as a baking mixture or sugar solution. Because they are not adult fungi but merely spores, they remain alive despite desiccation. Yeast itself dies if kept in a dry state for a long time.

A kindred craft to baking is brewing—a craft whose products, some people would argue, are nearly as essential to man's well-being as dairy foods and bread. Wines and beers are notably various in texture and flavor; yet although scientists have studied them intensively, we do not know the exact reasons why one wine or beer is so very different from all others made by similar means. It is an interesting fact that biochemists can precisely define the quality and purity of an antibiotic produced industrially by microorganisms. And, given certain specific microorganisms grown in certain prescribed fashions, they can exactly duplicate the antibiotic under consideration. But they cannot do

anything similar with wine and beer. Brewing and wine-making have always been—and will remain—more nearly in the realm of the arts than in that of the sciences.

After the grapes from which most, though by no means all, wines are made have been crushed, the unfermented juice—called *must*—is a suitable medium for the growth of yeasts and molds. Because it is an acidic solution, bacteria do not grow in it. Traditionally, the microorganisms that ferment the must—a species of *Saccharomyces*—are present on the skins of the harvested grapes, having arrived there from the atmosphere. These are known as "wild" yeasts, because they have not been cultivated or modified by man. In modern times, however, a cultivated culture of yeast is added to the must, which is then kept in large vats and well aerated while the fungus goes to work on the sugar in the juice.

Up to a point, the yeast population grows rapidly and forms alcohol and carbon dioxide gas. In general, however, growth stops when the concentration of alcohol in the must has reached about 14 to 15 per cent; after this the yeast cells are killed off by the alcohol that they have produced, and fermentation ceases. That marks the end of the microbiological part of the wine-making process and the beginning of a second stage, during which the newly fermented wine is stored and permitted to age. Now it is at risk from any other stray microbes, which could easily spoil the flavor and quality of the maturing wine. It was Louis Pasteur who first examined this problem scientifically and made suggestions for overcoming it. What we now call pasteurization was again his chief recommendation, for he pointed out that if the wine is heated to 140°F for a few minutes after fermentation has been completed, alien microbes are killed without damaging the wine. He also emphasized that the use of pure yeast, free from bacterial contamination, and the maintenance of scrupulous cleanliness in all the wineries and breweries would go a very long way toward eliminating diseased wine and beer.

Beers are made from barley, which contains starch, a substance that yeasts cannot break down. Thus the first step in beer-making is to convert the starch to sugar. Barley will do this on its own account if left to germinate, for the conversion of stored starch to sugar is one of the first stages in the germination of this seed. So barley grains are allowed to germinate for a

little while. Then, when some of the starch has been converted to sugar, the barley is dried, and the dried, partly germinated barley is what we call *malt*. The next step is to grind the malt in water, boil it, and filter it. This results in a liquid that brewers call *wort,* which is next mixed with hops, to give the beer its characteristically bitter taste.

The brew is now ready for fermentation, which is started by the addition of a special kind of yeast belonging to a group called "beer yeasts." These fungi do not live free in nature, as do the wine yeasts, but have been bred by man through the course of centuries. Often spoken of as "tame" yeasts, they resemble their "wild" cousins about as much as an Alsatian dog resembles a Siberian wolf. A brewer's success has always been measured by his ability to cultivate a yeast that makes good beer and to transfer it from one brew to the next without contamination by wild undesirable microorganisms. Special types of tame yeast have therefore been developed as a result of many long years of breeding, according to basic principles that differ very little from those governing the breeding of horses or roses.

Through bacterial activity, beer and wine (and, indeed, other beverages, such as cider) can undergo a further transformation, which also results in a product useful to man: vinegar. The organisms responsible are a small group of bacteria, the acetic acid bacteria. What most gourmets consider the best wine vinegar is produced by the so-called "Orleans process," named after the French town of Orleans, where it originated. In this process, wooden casks are half-filled with wine and placed on their sides, with holes bored in the uppermost part of the cask to let the air in. With the air come the bacteria, which float into the cask and form a thin layer on the surface. The bacteria get the energy that they need for growth and reproduction by converting the wine alcohol into the dilute solution of acetic acid that we call *vinegar* (from the French words *vin aigre,* meaning "sour wine").

In all the processes that we have mentioned so far, invisible organisms actually build up

The popular unfermented juice from Concord grapes (left) retains a fresh-grape flavor. But juice exposed to yeasts ferments and changes into wine. Right: Madeiran peasants using an ancient stone press to squeeze the juice from grapes. Above: frothy surface of fermenting juice that will become port wine.

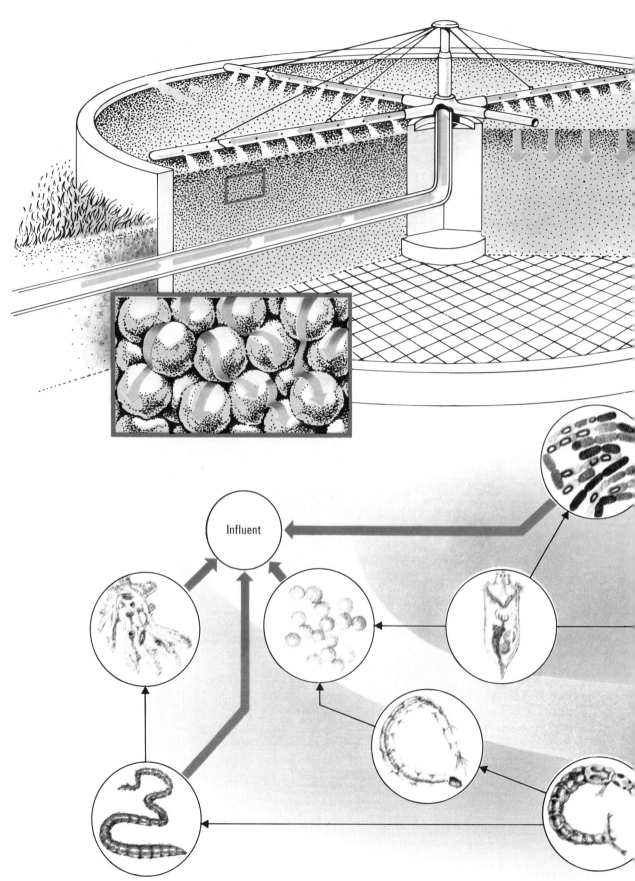

Influent

A Simple Food Web in a Trickle-Filter System

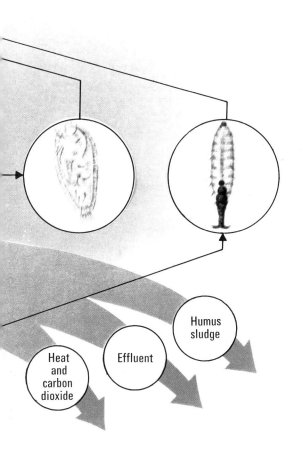

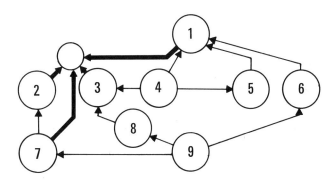

1 Bacteria
2 Amoeba
3 Yeast
4 Rotifer
5 Ciliate
6 Moth fly larva
7 Worm
8 Fly larva
9 Midge larva

Cutaway view of a trickle-filter (above, left) shows raw sewage sprayed onto a hardcore bed. Here, bits of crushed rock (rectangular inset) acquire a sewage coat supporting a food web of tiny organisms (below left). Worms, amoebas, yeast, and bacteria consume sewage and provide food for rotifers, ciliates, and insect larvae. The organisms turn noxious effluent into clear water and other equally harmless waste products.

Heat and carbon dioxide

Effluent

Humus sludge

different and highly desirable substances by breaking *down* the substances from which they are derived. So the microorganisms, you might say, are mighty creators as well as destroyers. In no area of modern life does man profit more immediately from this paradox than in the area of sanitation—especially in the purification of water and the disposal of sewage. These are major problems for every modern city, with its insatiable thirst for water and its fantastic ability to produce sewage. For a city of 1 million people, the inflow of water may be as high as 625,000 tons a day, and the output of sewage as much as 500,000 tons a day. Water-treatment plant can remove sewage wastes from water and render it safe to drink; and it is vital that this should be done, for many cities these days are forced to use water that has been discharged through the sewers of other cities farther upstream. Untreated water is dangerous, because of the poisons and some harmful microorganisms in it. So we get rid of them both by means of other, airborne microorganisms.

The first stage in water purification is the removal of solid nonorganic debris—a mechanical operation in which microorganisms play no part. Their role is all-important, however, when it comes to cleansing the water of human and other animal wastes and of virulent microorganisms. This can be done in any one of several ways. In one method of sewage treatment, untreated sewage is run into large tanks, where it remains for up to four weeks. Solid residues sink to the bottom and are periodically removed for burning or burial. Meanwhile, the organic sewage is fermented by bacteria, which produce two gases, carbon dioxide and methane. These bacteria float into the tanks from the atmosphere, but they do not need oxygen to keep alive and multiply. Gradually, all the wastes are converted into carbon dioxide and methane, and in some systems the methane is burned to provide energy for local heating and cooking. The dangerous bacteria sink to the bottom of the tank with the solid debris and are removed and burned.

In another possible method of treatment, the purifying job is done by bacteria that do need oxygen and that accomplish their task in the airy crevices of a six-foot deep bed of crushed rock. Untreated sewage is sprayed onto the top of this enormous filtering device, and as it trickles down through the bed, the wastes stick to the rocks. Naturally microorganisms floating in from the air grow in profusion on these wastes. Additional air is forced through the bed from below. And so the sewage is rendered harmless by what is in effect a miniature food chain. The waste matter is attacked first by slime-forming bacteria, filamentous bacteria, and filamentous fungi; these are in turn eaten by protozoans, which are in their turn eaten by minute animals. By breaking down the wastes to provide themselves with energy, all these hungry creatures leave nothing but harmless carbon dioxide and water. And the water that they leave is thoroughly safe for human consumption.

These and several other sewage-treatment techniques all operate on the same familiar principle of biodegradation. Any sewage-treatment plant, whatever its special methods, is in essence just a collecting place for sewage, where the microbes can most effectively do their work of breaking down organic substances. It is fortunate for us that the microorganisms are so efficient, because a high proportion of our daily water supply depends on them. There are few more instructive experiences than a tour of a sewage plant. If you have seen the state of the water when it comes in for purification and are handed a glass of it to drink after it emerges from the process, you may momentarily wish you were somewhere else. But you need not hesitate. You can be sure that the busy creatures of the invisible world have done their job.

So if the story of microorganisms sometimes seems overfull of grim details of diseases and destruction, we should remember that the relationship of one organism to another is very finely balanced, and that the damage done to other organisms by the microbes is the exception rather than the rule. In the main, peaceful and mutually beneficial coexistence is the order of the day.

What marks the microorganisms apart from all other life on earth is the strangeness of their tiny existence. This other-worldliness has proved a continual source of fascination to microbiologists ever since Anton van Leeuwenhoek observed and wrote about microscopic life 250 years ago. Although microorganisms impinge upon every aspect of our everyday lives, they seem to us to be a little magical, a little miraculous. The medieval alchemist who longed to change lead into gold would surely have thought himself far along toward his goal if he had been given a private glimpse of the invisible living creatures that can cause and cure disease, turn grape juice into wine, or render poisonous wastes harmless. Even today we marvel at their powers, especially their power to survive. Faced with new situations and new perils, they reproduce so quickly that evolution occurs in a matter of hours rather than thousands of years, and a new breed of microbe almost inevitably manages to overcome or sidestep any dangers.

There is great concern today about our earth. Many fear that it is heading for disaster, whether from the misuse of technology, the destruction of ecological relationships, the population explosion, or the possibility of atomic warfare. No matter what calamity man brings on himself and other visible forms of life, however, the surface of this planet would have to glow red hot, or lie buried under hundreds of feet of ice, before the microorganisms would be cheated out of their unique inheritance.

Crop-spraying from the air controls pests and weeds including microscopic fungi. But while man can exterminate big animals, his invisibly tiny enemies defy total destruction. Microbes— whether hostile, harmless, or beneficial to us—are the most prolific and adaptable of all organisms living on this earth.

Index

Page numbers in *italics* refer to illustrations or captions to illustrations

Picture Credits

Key to position of picture on page: (B) bottom, (C) center, (L) left, (R) right, (T) top; hence (BR) bottom right, (CL) center left, etc.

Artist Credits